Teach Your Preschooler to Read

DONALD G. EMERY, Ph.D.

SIMON AND SCHUSTER · NEW YORK

1 2 3 4 5 6 7 8 9 10

LIBRARY OF CONGRESS CATALOGING IN PUBLICATION DATA
EMERY, DONALD G.
    TEACH YOUR PRESCHOOLER TO READ.

    INCLUDES BIBLIOGRAPHICAL REFERENCES.
    1. READING (PRESCHOOL)   I. TITLE.
LB1140.5.R4E46   372.4'1   75-11917
ISBN 0-671-22069-1

To the memory of Lota Snyder Emery

CONTENTS

INTRODUCTION

The failure of schools to teach all children to read is the great national issue in education. It is our most persistent and costly educational problem. Though more research has been conducted and reported on reading than on any other educational topic over the past fifty years, schools still fail to teach 25 percent of our children to read successfully.

The quality of a child's entire life is depressed when he is a handicapped reader. It costs the nation hundreds of millions of dollars unnecessarily each year for failing readers to repeat a school grade. The lifetime earning power of the poor reader is severely reduced. He will pay little toward the support of public services and will contribute little to the life of his community. Failure to teach all children to read saps the vitality of the nation.

In spite of the distress that poor reading causes the child, the anxiety that it evokes in parents, and the frustration that it produces in the teacher, little new progress is being made in teaching beginning readers. Something is fundamentally wrong when, in spite of experiments and research with reading methods and materials, tens of thousands of school children every year fail to learn the basic skills of reading.

There is an obvious but persistently overlooked cause for the nation's reading problem. That cause is carefully identified in this book. Surprisingly, this fresh analysis shows that the root of the problem and its correction lie not in the school but in the home! This revelation in no way defends the failure of our schools. It explains the failure, and it calls attention to the real way for nearly all children to learn to read successfully. Fresh thinking,

NOTE: The use of the masculine personal pronoun "he" throughout this book is intended as a matter of convenience for the author and should be understood to refer to young children of both sexes who will share equally from the efforts of understanding and motivated parents to help them become beginning readers at a preschool age.

unfettered by the historic constraints that have made earlier efforts unproductive, is provided. Based on my thirty years of experience as teacher, school administrator, professor and parent, this book presents a factual and common-sense exposition showing that the correction of the national reading problem lies with parents in homes during the preschool years. This may seem to be a radical declaration to many teachers and parents. But those not already brainwashed by the myth about age six being the time for beginning reading will recognize the logic of the analysis and will use the straightforward help offered in this book. No other avenue can eradicate the tragedy imposed on many children by our historic patterns of teaching reading.

A traditional handicap in analyzing the problem has been the restraints on thinking imposed by reading specialists. They have confined their thinking within artificially imposed boundaries. They have *presumed* that a child must be at least six years old to learn to read; that a teacher must do the teaching; and that the teaching must be done *in school* with small groups of children. These presumptions have denied and prevented objective analyses and the action required. None of the presumptions is true. In fact, their continued operation has been a large part of the problem. These beliefs have caused beginning reading to be offered too late for most children. This book is a fresh look at the problem free of the blinders that have led too often to just tinkering with the improvement of reading instead of seeking the root of the problem.

Educators for years have exercised a kind of tunnel vision, looking only at children in school and reading methods and materials *there*. Because almost all study involved children in school, it was easy for stereotyped thinking about the problem to arise. As a career educator, but not a reading specialist, I have been close enough to the problem to be keenly aware of it, but not so intensely oriented as to become entrapped by the usual thinking. Early training as a physiologist and as a psychologist alerted me to other factors essential to looking beyond in-school instruction to the preschool child, his readiness and capacity for learning to read. Further, as a professor I have been acquainted with the shortcomings of reading preparation for teachers in training. As a classroom teacher and as a superintendent of schools, I came to recognize that the typical parent can carry out unsophisticated but logical steps needed to develop beginning-reading success in preschool-age children.

My intense inquiry into the problem began with some simple propositions. If all children can learn the oral-speech code well by age four, why can't they learn the printed code more easily? If parents, regardless of educational level, can teach very young children to talk fluently, why can't parents be successful in teaching beginners to read? If children are naturally interested in printed language long before they enroll in school, does not delaying instruction in reading actually damage and depress their interest or create anxiety about learning to read later? Forthrightly facing these questions resulted in the preparation of this book.

Most parents will understand this book. They will recognize its pertinence to their own family life. It will provide the help they need to teach beginning reading at home. Some will continue to believe the myth about age six and reading. Common sense tells us differently. So do the data presented in this book. A parent made conscious of the stages followed in teaching the child to *speak* will know that one can expect success in teaching preschoolers to *read*. In fact, the parent must not risk the two-year wait before a school can try its hand at teaching the child to read.

The only way to guarantee beginning-reading success is to start the child as a preschooler at home, as described in this book. No kindergarten, preschool or day-care center is able or interested in really teaching your child beginning reading. Nor is any federal- or state-directed or -supported program, regardless of tax funding, going to assure that your child really will learn to read. Unless you decide to act as a concerned parent, you are knowingly taking the one-in-four gamble the present system offers—regardless of your child's I.Q.

As a teacher and an administrator in rural, urban and suburban communities, I have observed surprising differences in reading achievement among students of comparable ability. The range of differences would hardly be expected in a single school or school district, yet they are there. These differences are unexpected when one recalls that the teachers of these pupils come from the same general teacher-education colleges, that the basal reading books used are the same or similar, and the methods and time allowed are comparable. Though a slight advantage may be ascribed to higher-I.Q. pupils, reading research does not demonstrate that brighter children learn to read consistently better than the less-bright pupils. The reason for differences in beginning-reading success lies not in the school but in the home!

School districts in which a greater proportion of children learn to read well share the fact of high parental interest in their children and in the school. Such parents not only are alert and responsive to the language interests of their preschool-age children, but they continue that interest during the early school years. As superintendent of two of America's most affluent and successful school districts, I observed this fact year after year. The primary reason for more reading failures in the central cities and urban centers is not the schools themselves, but the homes from which the children come and the lack of language orientation for many of these children before they ever get to school.

As soon as children have a reasonable mastery of oral language, they become curious about printed language. Every home has the evidence at hand and most four-year-olds exhibit it. This curiosity must be responded to if natural language development is to continue. To delay and put aside the child's expressed interest is a major disservice to the child and to the nation. When parents act to guarantee beginning-reading success at home, it does not relieve schools of their responsibility to extend and refine beginning reading into intermediate- and advanced-reading skills. This book will help parents think through their responsibility and opportunity, and it will guide them in doing something about it.

D. G. E.
Westchester County
New York

1

The Myth,
Our Language
and Literacy

How well a child learns to read shapes the child's life. Yet, which children learn to read and how well are as unsure as a lottery. One fourth of the nation's children don't learn to read well enough to use the skill practically. Eighteen million adult Americans read so poorly that they are functional illiterates.

If one out of every four television sets, refrigerators and automobiles manufactured wouldn't function properly when delivered, immediate corrective actions would be demanded. Yet, when one out of four children passing through our schools turns out as a disabled human being, unable to read well enough to succeed in our society, we tolerate it. We have debated fruitlessly too long about *how* to teach reading best. We don't need more argument about methods. We need to focus our attention and energy on *when* reading is first taught. It is *when* we first teach reading, rather than *how* we teach, that has produced much of this national problem.

REJECTED PARENTS

The natural interest of parents in beginning reading has been rejected too long. When parents want to help their preschool child with beginning reading, they are consistently discouraged by teachers. Parents are told to leave the teaching of reading to the schools. Parents are warned that they may confuse their children, damage their vision, or make them bored with school itself. They are warned that the little success that may be possible would not help much anyway. Teachers act as if the teaching of reading were a mystique that only they understand. Hard-to-convince parents are put down with semitechnical jargon about subskills, letter reversals and digraphs. Most well-intentioned parents are scared off.

Even when children are in school and encounter trouble with reading, concerned parents are rebuffed. Too often, parents are counseled that if they will just be patient until the end of first grade or into the second or even the third grade, all will be well. Too often it isn't. The proportion of reading failures remains distressingly high. Yet school personnel persist in putting the blame elsewhere. They point to inner-city residence, minority-race handicaps, Spanish-speaking homes, et cetera, as nonschool reasons for in-school reading failures.

Under real pressure for an accounting, teachers often claim that a child is "dyslexic." This pseudo-scientific term is used to slide the blame from the school over to the child or to the family. Dyslexia has become a smoke screen too often offered as an "explanation" of why a child can't read. But, it is not a real explanation. It does not describe a cause-and-effect relationship as in saying a particular virus causes measles. The term only means that a child can't read well and *the school doesn't know why!* Even a national commission, after a year of discussion, couldn't come to agreement on what the term means.[1] The best consensus within the commission was that dyslexia means that a child has an *unexplained* difficulty in learning to read despite conventional instruction, adequate intelligence and normal socio-economic opportunity. In other words, they didn't know why. Some teachers, frustrated with lack of success in teaching children to read, fall back on the dyslexia cliché with parents, to reduce their own guilt feelings.

Actually, many teachers have little preparation for the teaching of beginning reading—much less sophisticated insights into diagnostic or prescriptive techniques. Few teachers in training are professionally prepared to meet the challenge of teaching beginning reading to twenty-five to forty first-graders.

The effective teaching of reading is our largest national educational problem. We are long overdue in correcting it. The root of the problem is not money. The root is that we underestimate the ability of the preschool child and we start *too late* to teach beginners to read. We teach beginning reading at the wrong time and in the wrong place. Until we confront these propositions, failures will continue. Children are naturally ready at age four, and an interested parent can successfully teach beginning reading at home. Until parents decide that reading skills can be initially developed at home before the child enters school, millions of school children will continue to become nonreading adults.

THE PERPETUATED MYTH

Almost any primary-grade teacher will tell you that children aren't ready to learn to read until they are six years old. Ask why, and you will get some fascinating replies—all the way from, "Everybody knows that," to "You will only make it more difficult for them later if you try." You are not likely to hear a real reason or a research-based reply. Not only does the entrenched myth say that a child needs to be at least six, it also presumes that the child must be in school to learn to read.

Several generations of teachers in training have been raised on this myth. That is what their textbooks reported; that is what their professors taught them. The teachers, in turn, passed the myth along as truth to parents. In fact, better-educated parents who are easily able to help children read early are the very ones who often refrain because they know that teachers object to early home reading help. Lesser-educated parents, being less aware of the school's warnings, often have provided useful help to their children.

The delaying of beginning-reading instruction until the first grade imposes a handicapping two-year wait on a child who already has considerable speech mastery and is naturally ready earlier to learn to read. There is no proof that reading instruction must wait until age six. The evidence is quite contrary and favors an early, at-home beginning.

It has not been proven that a child must wait until age six to really learn to read. The myth has effectively discouraged large-scale, organized programs that would demonstrate successful instruction with pre-age-six groups. There has been the complication of studying four-year-olds outside schools, and the professional has often been blinded by his prejudiced notion that parents can't provide initial reading instruction at home. Hence, serious studies of four-year-olds learning to read have seldom been attempted. Yet, positive evidence is available.

Where did the age-six fixation come from? College textbooks commonly advise that children should be six years old to begin reading. Unfortunately, such advice often quotes just another textbook that says the same thing. Was there a beginning? This fixation has been with us for almost fifty years now. The real genesis of the age-six myth must be identified for what it is.

HOW WE GOT THAT WAY

Since the middle of the nineteenth century, children have received formal instruction in reading at whatever age they were required to begin attending school. However, in our earlier colonial history, the responsibility for education was fixed on the parent *and* on the schoolmaster. Early laws, such as those of the town councilmen in the state of Massachusetts two hundred years ago, placed on them the responsibility and the authority "to see that the children can read and understand the principles of religion and the capital laws of the country."[2] This authority reached into the home as well as into the school. Learning to read was not always viewed as a unique responsibility of the school. The progressive failure of schools to teach reading over the past two decades makes it imperative that a new resource— the parent—enter the picture.

The Influence of Compulsory Attendance Laws

State compulsory school-attendance laws began to appear soon after 1850. By 1900, the average beginning age for required school attendance in the twenty-six states having such laws was eight years. Only one state had an age-six law. By 1935, the average age had dropped to 7.3 years. Sixteen states still set age eight. Today, age six is clearly the predominant age for the beginning of compulsory school attendance. Our current practice of beginning reading instruction at age six exists *because that is when the child has to come to school.*

Compulsory school-attendance laws apply to the first grade— not to kindergarten. Kindergarten education has always been an optional opportunity, though often provided at public expense. The history of kindergarten as an educational unit developed from a totally different rationale than just a "backing down," over time, of the lower compulsory-attendance age.

If kindergartens had arisen as a result of states finally lowering the school beginning age to five years, we could logically expect to find beginning-reading instruction universally at that level. We don't. The American kindergarten developed separately from, but parallel to, the public-school movement over the past century. The philosophy of the kindergarten has been unique to its German origin (*kindergarten*—i.e., "child garden") and has continued to include much of its original thesis, which allowed the child to follow his own natural development. More lately, planned play and socializing experiences have been added.

The first kindergarten was instituted in 1837, in Blankenburg, Germany, and the first kindergarten in the United States, a German-speaking edition, was established in 1856 in Watertown, Wisconsin. This new child institution spread rapidly, and by 1900 about 30 percent of the five-year-olds of that year were enrolled. Today, kindergartens enroll over two million children— more than 60 percent of the age-five population. Most states have legislation authorizing kindergartens, and many offer financial assistance to local school districts that choose to operate this kind of early school unit.

More recently, attempts have been made to fit the kindergarten more effectively to the first grade. So far, the general result has been adding a variety of "readiness" activities to the kindergarten's one-half school day. Formal schooling still literally begins with the first grade.

If compulsory school-attendance laws required children to enroll in first grade at nine or eight years of age, that is when they were taught to read. When the law specified age seven and finally age six, that is when reading instruction began. However, age six was "the end of the line" for moving the compulsory school-attendance age lower. It collided with the already well-established, but optional, kindergarten movement, having its own philosophy and activities for serving five-year-olds.

Since kindergartens are voluntary, not all five-year-olds enroll. Many school districts still do not provide this opportunity. Since not all children attend kindergarten, educators and school boards have felt that reading instruction should wait until the first grade. Otherwise, there would be two types of first-graders—those with some reading instruction from kindergarten and others with none. *Failing to teach beginning reading before age six is an historical accident without a scientific foundation.*

The Influence of Testing

Standardized testing in schools is a product of this century. The testing movement began about 1910, and within twenty years hundreds of "standardized" tests were on the market, covering every conceivable school subject. Standardized simply meant that the proposed test had been tried out on trial groups of children and its difficulty level determined. The difficulty level could be expressed as either a *mental age* or a *grade norm.*

Reading and its related skills of spelling, handwriting, vocabulary, punctuation, et cetera, were a favorite testing field. The high
incidence of first-grade failure and required repeating of the
grade was often caused by reading failures, and such children
were heavily tested.

The testing movement generated the other major condition
that trapped us in the idea that age six was the correct time for
beginning reading. By finding out by trial and experiment at
what age a child could usually answer or pass a sample test
question correctly, a *mental age* could be assigned as its "difficulty level." Accordingly, a child of eight and a half years might
be expected to solve a particular arithmetic problem or read
without error a particular literary passage. Therefore, successful
completion of these "standardized" test items was felt to prove a
mental age of 8.5 years (or the school year and month appropriate to that chronological age—3.5). This technique permitted
assigning a single mental-age score or school-grade level as a
result for the whole test. Child performance on tests popularly
came to be reported in terms of the mental age demonstrated by
test performance. The simplicity of a single score for a test—
either as mental-age or grade-level designation—led to arbitrary
and categorical thinking about and labeling of children. Many of
the standardizing procedures in constructing tests did not justify
the arbitrary way scores were used.

By the 1920s, test literature and conversation were heavily
weighted with mental-age phraseology. By 1930, a "mental age"
of between six and seven years was being reported as the level
below which *less-rapid progress* was made in learning to read.
An unjustified attitude began to emerge that a mental age of six
or more years *was necessary* for learning to read.

In 1931, a study in beginning reading conducted in suburban
Winnetka, Illinois, was destined to overly influence thinking
about when reading should be taught first. Carleton Washburne,
the school superintendent, and Mabel Morphett conducted the
study.[3] After analyzing children's performance against the generally high standards expected in that favored community, they

concluded that a mental age of six and a half years was the *optimal time* at which reading instruction should begin. Studies in the next few years called for starting even later.

A general conclusion was forming from studies based on groups of children in *school settings*. At best, the findings were appropriate only to those situations and the forms of instruction then used. The age-six fixation did not emerge from studies trying to determine whether children less than age six could learn to read. Further, the studies were only saying that older children seemed to learn easier in group school settings—not that younger children could not learn to read.

By 1935, a mental age of six to six and one half was established in educational thinking as *the* age when reading instruction should begin. Few studies have been carried out directly with five- and four-year-olds. Physiologists clouded the picture further with estimates that the sensory organs and the neurological systems of young children *might not* be adequate for the disciplined task of reading as it was then taught in schools. Little definitive study with five- and four-year-olds was attempted.

As time went on, few educators or researchers were willing to go against what had come to be the conventional wisdom about age six for beginning reading. The pseudo-scientific halo of "mental age" had been made to fit the compulsory school-attending age of six years. One wonders what would have been the result if the testing movement had occurred fifty years earlier. The few studies that produced contrary results were so out of step with the new professional credo that they were neglected or ignored. Age six became locked into professional thinking. Teachers progressively persuaded parents to believe the same thing. They still do.

READING—THE ESSENTIAL SKILL

Speaking, writing and reading are uniquely human skills. Mastering each is fundamental. How well one succeeds largely determines the kind of person, citizen, worker, spouse and neighbor he will become. The greatest challenge to a child and the greatest benefit to his life lie in learning our oral and written codes of communication.

If the child is successful, a superior social, economic and personal world will be open to him. Failure to master these skills usually consigns a person to an ordinary and pedestrian life.

We take our language too much for granted. Job and business success, personal and recreational pleasures, friendships and family relations, and one's view of life often are determined by language skills. To help a child learn to speak and read is the greatest gift of a parent. To neglect either is the greatest dereliction.

All parents naturally expect to teach their children to speak. Strangely though, teaching the same child to read is delayed, neglected within the family, and finally turned over to a school, often too late. *The parent who taught the very young child to speak will be successful in helping the preschool child to learn to read.* Only when children can speak with reasonable mastery can they make progress with the somewhat more difficult reading code. The child's vocabulary of spoken words will be the primary resource for first learning to read. By age four a child's command of speech automatically triggers an interest in printed words and reading. The signs are clear, but they often go unnoticed—largely because the age-six myth blinds parents to reality in their own home.

Any interested parent can help a child learn to read. First he or she needs to recall how the child learned to speak at home and to think through what is involved in learning to read. With minimal understanding but consistency the parent can successfully begin to teach reading. Later chapters provide a complete orientation. Children at four have a natural curiosity about how reading works, and they are eager to begin. They have a large oral vocabulary. Their sensory organs are sufficiently developed. They want to learn to read. They can learn to read. Those given help do learn to read.

The usual two-year delay forced on children now, until the first grade, is an unfortunate tradition rooted in a myth. The delay is not of the children's choosing—they are ready. Parents must be interested and willing. Parents who have already helped children to learn to speak can help them learn to read before they enter school. Parents' early reading help at home will assure reading success for the child and the school later. Delay until age six is the real reading villain in this nation.

Reading means the ability to interpret symbols that stand for objects, actions or qualities. The symbols can be understood only when they represent information or experience already in the knowledge of the reader. Essentially, reading is the process of decoding—that is, assigning an agreed meaning mentally to code symbols. Usually we think of reading as interpreting or getting meaning from printed symbols such as those on this page. However, decoding a group of letters is only one form of reading. We "read" road-sign symbols, a thermometer, stock market quotations, recipes and other codes. Each act of reading requires us to attach a *pre-agreed meaning* to pictures, numbers, letters or other symbols.

Code systems change. In one lifetime we think of our language as a fixed system. But languages change over the centuries. Most of us can read English printed three hundred years ago, but few of us can read English written six hundred years ago.

Man, no doubt, first acted out meanings by using gestures to convey information about events and activities. Even today, our tendency to make gestures demonstrates a natural disposition to represent reality by symbols in order to speed up or emphasize the meanings we want to convey. None of us can fully appreciate the long and difficult process required to construct a crude spoken language. Laboriously, over centuries, Stone Age humans must have agreed on certain meanings for different calls, cries and grunts in regard to food, hunting, danger, shelter, et cetera. They gradually began to communicate through these sounds. Being able to use agreed-on sounds (words) was a great convenience. Learning the agreed-on meaning for code symbols is the heart of *reading*. Such activity is possible, practical and interesting to young children in the home.

Though anthropologists estimate that man has been in his present state of physical development, including his much underused brain capacity, for at least fifty thousand years, it has only been in the last five thousand years that written codes have been used. It was an intellectual triumph when man realized that marks could be made to stand for sounds which in turn represented real things.

Our English language, using twenty-six Roman alphabet letters to represent various sounds that can be uttered together as words and can be arranged in sentences to convey thought, is a remarkable achievement. It is not, though, as easy a system to learn to read as Italian, Spanish or Russian, in which languages there is a more direct correspondence (simplified spellings) between sounds spoken and the letters that represent them.

IN THE BEGINNING

The English language today is the result of linguistic evolution. English, as we know it, has been shaped by many influences through the centuries. There is not even agreement on the number of separate sounds used in English, although usually there are forty-four counted in acceptable speech. If we had forty-four agreed-upon separate letters or symbols for the forty-four sounds, learning to read would be much easier. Unfortunately, the twenty-six letters of our alphabet can be combined in dozens of ways to represent these sounds. It is this quirk of fate and language evolution that makes the later stages of learning to read more difficult. For beginners it is important that the logical and consistent aspects of reading be emphasized. The inconsistencies should be delayed to avoid confusion.

If we look briefly into the history of the English language, we will have a better appreciation of why it is not phonetically consistent—that is, why its sounds don't correspond directly to the letter or letter groups which represent them. History accounts for many of these irregularities. English was strongly influenced originally by its Germanic originators; by Latin through its role in shaping the European Romance languages; and by French during a conquest of England by the Normans.

Originally, English was the language of Germanic tribes from the continent of Europe who, about 450 A.D., invaded the island later to be known as England. These tribes, the Angles and the Saxons, subdued the original inhabitants, the Celts. The Anglo-Saxons being in control, their language, Englisc, spread. In the eleventh century the successful invasion and conquest of the island by the Normans made French the official written and legal language. However, Englisc continued as the commonly spoken tongue. Norman rule introduced both French itself and Latin influences that already had Romanized that language earlier. Over several generations, the Norman French language blended with the German tongue of the Anglo-Saxons to become early English. Modern English dates from the 1500s and has continued to change up to the present day. The influence of history on English is clear, and it accounts for some of the problems encountered in learning to read.

HUMAN SPEECH

Learning to speak a language is a universal trait of the nearly four billion inhabitants of the earth. Universality of speaking is the strongest evidence that man's brain is naturally disposed to creating and interpreting symbolic codes. Man's brain capacity and ability to articulate coded sounds are distinctly superior traits over all animal forms—even more so than man's erect carriage and opposing thumb and fingers. *Homo sapiens*—that is, "wise man"—is an accurate scientific label for man, because of his language ability and his skill at abstract reasoning.

About 70 percent of the earth's inhabitants speak one or more of only thirteen major languages. These fall into groups ranging from about 65 million speaking Italian to over 700 million speaking Chinese or one of its dialects. About 350 million are English-speaking.[4] If all the little-known tribal languages of only a few thousand active speakers in Africa, Australia, North America, etcetera, are included, the total number of spoken "languages" approaches 2,800. Man has been remarkably ingenious in devising a myriad of coded systems for communicating.

Using language is such an integrated and natural process in our lives that we forget what a remarkable achievement it is. Without written language, even our most elementary activities could not be carried out. We depend on it for such usual activities as driving in traffic, shopping for groceries, paying bills, making phone calls, leaving notes and writing friends.

The ability to speak is developed first through a one-to-one direct association between a young learner and another person. A young child only develops functional speech after an intensive exposure to vocal language for two or three years. Usually the mother is the one who develops the skill in the child—regardless of her own educational level. It is the child's oral vocabulary and ability to talk freely that make him ready to learn to read. This point occurs long before age six.

ILLITERACY AND ITS PRICE

A personal command of language being so important, we might expect nearly all adults to read and write. Not so! Millions of English-*speaking* people have not learned to read and write. A major reason within the language itself is its many phonetically arbitrary spellings. However, these complications are not sufficient to deter most from learning to read. Slightly more than one half of the adult population of the world are not functionally literate. That is, they cannot read or write their own language well enough (if at all) to use it as a practical tool in their everyday lives.

Around the world, according to UNESCO statistics, 810 million adults are classified as illiterate. That actually is an increase of 100 million above the data of just twenty years ago, as the world's population has soared.

In 1971 and 1972 the National Reading Center in Washington, D.C., sponsored two American literacy surveys. By population sampling techniques the Center determined how many adults could read common examples of printed matter such as newspaper ads, driver-license application questions, long-distance-phone dialing instructions, et cetera. The surveys showed that at least 18 million Americans age sixteen and over were not functionally literate; they could not read well enough to meet the ordinary literacy demands of life. They have reading problems every day. Nearly one of every six adult Americans is handicapped this way at the very time when unskilled and semiskilled jobs are rapidly disappearing in society.

Among children, the percentage having reading difficulty is comparable to that in the adult world. U. S. Office of Education statistics indicate that one child in five has a reading handicap. In the central cities, two of every five are handicapped readers. Regular newspaper stories in metropolitan areas attest to the failure of schools to develop functional reading skills in many children. If only 5 percent of the 45 million children enrolled in the nation's elementary and secondary schools have to repeat a grade—or extend their time in school primarily due to reading and language disability—the estimated cost of repeating is nearly two billion dollars annually.

Every year poor readers are graduated from the nation's high schools. As a result, an estimated five million young adults are out of school and unable to obtain any but the most menial jobs. In the national work force, up to one fourth can be classified as disabled readers, to the extent that they could not accept a job promotion if it required reasonable reading skill. The total penalty paid by the individual, by society, by the family and by the national economy for nonreading is incalculable.

Introducing beginning reading at home should be a priority

obligation of every parent. First, good speech must be developed. Then, reading must be started before the school years. Since the school often fails, the parent must act to assure reading success.

A LOOK AHEAD

What is this national reading problem? It could be a matter of when we start, of how we start, of who does the job or of where it is done. When and where we start have been set by tradition. It is at age six and in the first grade. How we start has been a continuing debate for years and is reported in a later chapter. Tradition dictates that instruction in reading should be provided only by teachers—not by parents. The harsh facts about the national failure in the teaching of reading should make us severely question these assumptions and our traditional practices. This book does that.

The following chapters show that basic reading should and can be taught by parents at home, beginning ideally with four-year-olds. Further, the learning situation needed for positive results cannot be provided in institutionalized preschools, day-care centers or kindergartens. Nor can we expect primary teachers to substantially change the reading record already disgracing many schools. Too many are ill-prepared and will act too late to help many children. The broad, entrenched first-grade curriculum will continue to prevent the real time and emphasis that learning to read demands.

There is no more practical way for a young child to begin learning to read than with the help of an interested adult at home. The parent, untrained as a teacher, has been almost solely responsible for teaching the child, at age three, to speak effectively. The parent must go on to the next step at age four and begin the child's grasp of printed language and reading. A further two-year delay is unnecessary and harmful. The national reading picture can be changed significantly only by the parent at home before the child starts to school. The typical school is unable to change

its approach to beginning reading enough to make up for the loss
of interest, natural readiness and early reading mastery that can
be developed at ages four and five, at home. The answer to our
national reading problem lies there, not in our schools.

2

Learning
to Talk –
Grasping
the Great Idea

Speaking is a muscular skill and must be learned. Any motor skill
must be acquired, in large part, through practice, repetition and
refinement. Learning to ride a bicycle, hitting a golf ball well or
bowling expertly are small feats compared to learning to manage
one's own vocal apparatus so that communicative language is
produced.

Learning to speak doesn't "just happen," even though children
around the world follow a similar pattern in doing it. Probably no
skill developed later will have been the object of such intense
concentration, time and effort!

The rate at which oral language is acquired is phenomenal
when we consider the complexity of the skill and the obstacles
overcome by the very young child in the process. A mere fifty
months elapse generally from birth to the time of basic mastery
of our oral code. Unbelievable!

ACQUIRING VOCABULARY

Though authorities do not agree on the size of a young child's
vocabulary, there are fairly accurate estimates. At about the
eleventh or twelfth month most children say their first word. This

is a real language milestone. This event follows several months of babbling while the infant is acquiring greater control over his or her vocal apparatus and is refining a repertoire of sounds. One-year-olds may have a vocabulary of three words. During subsequent stages we can expect these developments, on the average. Children at one and a half years can say about 22 words; at twenty-one months over 100 words; at two years 272 words; at two and a half 446 words; at three, 896; and at three and a half 1,222. At four years old children have a working vocabulary of 1,540 words.[1] On entering first grade—usually at age six—they will come to school with a vocabulary about twice that of age four.

A word cannot be *read* (that is, understood when presented in print) unless the child knows the meaning of that word when presented orally. A speaking vocabulary, therefore, is an essential prerequisite for learning to read. The average four-year-old knows hundreds of words. Accordingly, we must have other reasons for making him or her wait two more years before learning to read. Do we have such reasons?

We must distinguish between the vocabulary that a child can speak and the vocabulary he can recognize when it is used in his presence or in print. Typically, one's *use* vocabulary is much smaller than his *recognition* vocabulary. We frequently encounter words in print that we "know" but do not normally use in our speech and writing. Often we can grasp the meaning of a strange word from the context in which it is used.

Many recognition words may be alternates or synonyms for words we normally use. For example, the words *large* and *huge* may be in our use vocabulary, but we may also recognize synonyms when they are used by other people, such as *mammoth, enormous, colossal, gigantic,* and *prodigious.* Enlargement of vocabulary as one becomes more experienced or more educated is, in part, the acquisition of these alternate forms of common words. Our recognition vocabulary may be increased by variations of root words such as *sad, sadder, sadly, sadness* and *saddened.* Compound words made up of two already-known words provide another boost to vocabulary, as in the case of *housetop, horseman, handbook.* The difference between the number of words we use and those we recognize can be quite large. While the typical first-grader has a use vocabulary of at least three thousand words, he may have a recognition vocabulary of twice that number. Some authorities state that for adults there are as many as ten recognized words for each use word.[2]

Vocabulary estimates as reported by linguists are quite varied. Some put the four-year-old's vocabulary at over 5,000 words and the six-year-old's at 14,000.[3] In any event, the young child has a command of hundreds and hundreds of words as a basis for beginning reading.

We should remember that a core of words are used repeatedly in everyday conversation and ordinary writing. "The" is the most commonly used English word. The articles *a* and *an;* prepositions like *of, to* and *for;* common pronouns like *you* and *he;* and common verb forms like *am, is* and *have* recur again and again. In a running English narrative of 100,000 words only about 3,000 different words generally make up 95 percent of the entire copy. Of the ten most common words in English, one will occur in every four words of continuous English, on the average.[4]

Not only do we face the challenge of learning words and what they mean (semantics), we must learn how to fit the words together in a sentence (syntax) and the patterns of grammar that make our use of language easier and more consistent. A person acquires language skill over many years. The sooner children get started, once they are ready, the greater will be their skill and advantage in life.

Introducing reading naturally in the home and developing a basic success and confidence pattern before taking up spelling inconsistencies will help build a foundation for total success later. The first initiative and opportunity lie with the parent when the child's vocabulary has reached a reasonable maturity at age four.

IT'S A WORD WORLD

The world is saturated with words. We are bombarded daily by an unending gushing of words from the radio, television, newspapers, magazines, neighbors, fellow workers, family, et cetera. The daily circulation of newspapers in the United States exceeds sixty million copies. The number of new book titles issued in the United States runs to a hundred every day or well over thirty-five thousand annually. New magazines are formed at a rate of nearly seventy-five a year. Radio and television spew out billions of words annually. The young child contributes to this flood. It has been estimated that the typical four-year-old says about fifteen thousand words a day, or nearly five and one-half million words a year.[5]

The very young child can learn language only through exposure to the speech of others. Therefore, the verbal environment of the infant is all-important. The actions and interest of the parents in particular, and members of the household in general, are critical. The parent is the primary creator and shaper of the "word world" of the child. Unless language is a normal and continuing part of the home, the child will take much longer to grasp the over-all nature of language. Unless the child hears conversation regularly and is spoken to directly, he will be delayed in grasping the *idea of language* and in understanding that the sounds he hears and the facial expressions he sees repeatedly relate to him and the world around him. Language can be developed only in response to the verbal environment surrounding the child.

The child's first uttered word is relatively unimportant in and of itself, except for the ego gratification of parents. It is the over-all language orientation being stimulated that is important. A few weeks one way or the other in producing the first word do not necessarily indicate any particular level of intelligence for the child—or for his parents. However, children of parents having more favorable socioeconomic status tend to have higher measured I.Q.'s and tend to speak first words earlier, on the average. The I.Q. and language level may be a reflection of the over-all stimulating environment these parents create around children rather than pure native capacity.

Language development corelates directly with the quality of verbal stimulation present in the home. More talking of good tonal and grammatical quality to and around the child will hasten his own acquisition of correct and effective speech. Children who are neglected, ignored, left alone, not talked to and not made a part of the continuing family conversation develop speech much more slowly and with less quality. Many studies have demonstrated that children raised in institutions, in contrast to comparably matched children raised in family situations, have measured I.Q.'s at a lower level and a lesser command of speech. However, some interesting studies have also shown that it is the *quality of attention* directed to the child, whether it is done under parental or institutional care, that makes the real difference in acquiring language.

EARLY LANGUAGE DEVELOPMENT

In the early months of growth there appears to be a rough parallel between stages of physical development and stages of verbal development. It is as though the small body and mind can be preoccupied only with one or the other at a time. At least, the verbal development appears to proceed in stages with plateaus of delay and waiting.

The infant holding his head up is one of the early physical feats, at about the second to third month. The first noncrying, regular verbal activity—cooing and general vocalizing—begins then, as though the change in gravity in relation to the infant's vocal apparatus had freed sounds. At about six months the infant begins to sit unaided, a new achievement of physical control. Concurrently, there begins a period of babbling in which all kinds of sound are explored and intonational ability is refined, for about six months. Near the time of rising to his feet and standing alone, around the twelfth month, the infant also utters, for the first time, a recognizable word as if to emphasize a new level of maturity and independence. Between the fifteenth and eighteenth months the baby begins to walk alone and, in this period too, may announce his first words in twos or threes as a first declarative expression or command (minisentence). The verbal feats tend to follow on the heels of the significant physical feats. Both physical and verbal accomplishments develop a new sense of self-identification and power in the young child.

What goes on inside the mind of the infant as he is exposed to the swirl of language around him is unknown. However, it is logical to deduce that a definite *passive* language activity is present as he continues to hear language and observe the various behaviors of adults about him in relation to language. The earliest speech is not just imitation. In fact, the first words are probably spontaneous explosions of monosyllabic word utterances from some past exposure to words used over and over in his presence. One day the word was just there—probably as much a surprise to the child as to the parent. However, that word probably had been a part of the child's past verbal environment for some time, or it could not have popped out. Expectant parents may think a word or two has been uttered much earlier, but that is often their own attachment of meaning to an accidental syllable combination during babbling. Shortly, genuine imitation and repeating of words starts, and the child's vocabulary begins to expand through the parents' leading questions— "What's this?"; "Touch your nose"; and "Where is Daddy?" This parental behavior is aimed at developing both mental understanding and word expression. Soon the youngster will be asking, "Whadda?" for all kinds of objects that are around him. The more interesting and varied the environment, the more likely is the child to improve and increase vocabulary.

A period of special speech readiness, a so-called "teachable moment" in the life of a young child, occurs between the twelfth and eighteenth month. This is the time in which the child reaps the greatest harvest from parental time, interest and activity supporting speech development. From this impetus, the two-year-old child will have garnered a vocabulary of close to 300 words. Parental interest and help are critical in this period. Before the child is two years old, adjectives and adverbs will be in his vocabulary; *big, round, soft, fast, high,* and *loud* probably will be among them. This is the time when trips out of the house should be used to stimulate the child's language interest. These should be talking and conversational trips using the words for and explaining all kinds of things, places and actions.

During the second year, the child is very observant and aware of conversation around him. He will intently watch talking people. It is clear that he is trying to puzzle out this business of talking. In speech directed to him the child is first preoccupied with what a person *means* by his expressions, manner and gestures rather than what the words mean. It is the totality of the communication directed to the child, not just the words, that is being noted. The association of words with objects or actions comes later. Through long and repeated observation of facial expressions, pointings, gestures and words, the child progressively stores up cues about language and gradually builds a mental association between objects, actions and words. It is as if, having been exposed long enough, the "virus" of language finally infects the child; or, as with photographic film, when there is enough light exposure, an image is recorded.

Language meaning, in a global sense rather than in an individual-word sense, is the nature of the early perception of the young child. All the puzzling about language and the general grasping of the communication situation are passive language activities and are internal. Later, active language will be helped enormously by these stored-up experiences and observations. The parent's enrichment of the verbal environment is a most important language investment for the child; from it dividends will be reaped later.

In his own play the young child goes through three stages that bear on language. First, he will be involved in solitary play employing egocentric language primarily and is preoccupied with himself as an organism in the environment. In this play he will often talk to himself. He will name the things he is playing with and the relationship between them as a form of word practice. He will name absent objects or people in his speech. This monologue is most important practice and supplements the verbal experience being fostered by his parents. However, the parent can intervene occasionally in this solitary play to great advantage. The small child is definitely limited as to the degree of vocabulary he can independently exercise. The parent by asking questions and briefly joining in the play can extend and enrich the "self-conversation" beyond the vocabulary that would otherwise be used. The parent has an excellent opportunity to introduce adjectives and adverbs to supplement the child's predominantly noun vocabulary. The "big" truck. The "round" ball. The "new" hat. Each extends the vocabulary and understanding level and practice of the child.

Later, the child will engage in parallel play activity alongside other children but will operate mainly as though he were really alone most of the time. The language pattern will continue to be more like that of solitary play.

Finally, the child will have advanced enough emotionally and socially to successfully participate in group play including socialized language exchange that goes with it. Group play provides an exceptional opportunity for verbal practice and enhances the child's sense of growing utility and mastery of language.

EVERYTHING HAS A NAME

There is a special moment in the life of everyone who learns to speak. It is the time of the dawning of the understanding that *everything has a name* and that you can learn to say the name of the things you want to talk about! Later on, the same concept will occur in connection with printed language—that everything has a name and it can be written. This is a moment of true exhilaration, of genuine discovery, and it opens the floodgates so that a torrent of words can enter the mind. This is the great idea of human language! What an ingenious idea! How practical it is for human beings who are so mobile and adept at using so many things. Now yesterday's, last month's and last year's events and activities can be readily described. Could civilization itself have come about without this invention in language? Imagine the internal exhilaration from this realization for the young mind after being exposed so intensively for months to language repetition. All things have names! All these sounds must be the names of all these things!

When the child uses his first "Whadda?" for "What is that?" he has passed the point of the great realization about the names of things. His noun collection of names "takes off." This realization accounts for the dramatic increase in his vocabulary after eighteen months. The dawning of the nature of language has occurred. It is a small step then to the fact that actions have names, too (*jump, fall down, run*), and that characteristics of things even have names.

Helen Keller, the famous deaf-mute child, experienced the same discovery. A miracle was worked in developing language understanding and oral speech in Miss Keller. In her case instead of oral sounds the names of things were spelled out manually in her hand. Her ecstatic reaction at grasping the idea that all things have names was emotionally portrayed in the stage play *The Miracle Worker.*

Exactly how this language realization comes about is unknown. This gives rise to the belief that the human being to some degree has an inborn cerebral disposition for language acquisition and that it can be stimulated and awakened by a rich verbal environment—like a seed that will germinate and sprout if the right conditions of moisture and temperature are provided.

GESTURES—PLUS AND MINUS

Gestures are a natural aid in learning to talk. However, the use of gestures can be overdone and can depress proper language development.

All children go through the stage of gestures, pointing and a variety of sounds to get what they want before their grasp of language is good enough to be more direct and complete. If, after they have begun to acquire some speaking ability, they are permitted to continue to get what they want by using gestures and half speech, they will be led into poor and deficient language. Speech development will be delayed and restricted. Tolerating gestures, half words and other nonword utterances is one of the characteristics of the environment of the disadvantaged child, and it may be found in wealthy overindulging homes at the other extreme. Gestures are a form of, or an aid to, communication, but they are not speech.

An older child in the family may naturally become the interpreter for a younger one. In such instances, the young one does not have to use speech to make his wants known. In either event, the wise parent will progressively insist that the child say what it wants. Speech is useful as our primary means of communication. Gestures should not be permitted long in place of words when speech is being developed. With the motivation of the "want of the moment," the parent has an excellent opportunity to draw out the appropriate word or words, or to present for imitation the correct words, so that obtaining the object will also reinforce the use of correct words. It is important for the parent to tell the interpreting older child that both he and Mother must help Baby learn how to talk and that the older child should not say too quickly what Baby is asking for. Explain that Mother does know what Baby wants much of the time. Make it a game for both to see if Baby really knows the word yet.

Speaking is a vocal motor skill. It must be learned through example and much practice. The difference between the amount

of daily speaking practice of the at-home middle-income suburban child as compared with that of the inner-city or ghetto
child can be several-fold. In the course of a month the suburban
child gets thousands of more word practices than the other.
Finally, the measure of whether true speech is occurring is
whether the child can, with understanding of their meaning,
utter words to which another person, listening, will attach the
intended meaning.

WORK WITH WHAT YOU HAVE

A parent does not have to possess an excellent vocabulary to
provide a verbal environment for the young child. Every parent
must try. There are no mechanical substitutes. Television programs can be of some help in establishing the concept of verbal
communication. In no sense, however, should television be considered as a suitable substitute for a parent talking to his or her
child, or for family conversation in the presence of the child.

Limited speech ability in three- and four-year-olds is generally
caused by the absence of verbal stimulation in the home and by
parental neglect. The young child is quite disposed to and will
learn to talk within the limits of the interest, imagination and
work of parents helping him.

Dialects and accents of all kinds characterize the world of
English-speaking people. Speech patterns of parents who serve as
models for children vary greatly. Though grammar used in some
homes will be incorrect, the parent must go ahead and help the
child learn to speak in the mores of that household. The alterna-
tive is the greater danger, neglect of the child. Most homes
provide reasonable speech models. It is better that the child
grasp the idea of speech and learn to talk in his home and
neighborhood than that he become retarded in speech. Even as
the speaker of one language can learn another language later on,
under proper motivation, the child growing up with poor grammar and poor pronunciation can work out improvements in his

speech later. Many general motor skills must first be learned from amateurs, or people who don't show real proficiency themselves. The learner can work out improvements and corrections later by personal motivation or with the assistance of expert instruction. Parents often are the only available teachers even though they may not be ideal models.

So-called "Black English" has its own logic and structure and is well understood in many homes and neighborhoods having a concentration of poor blacks. Speakers of Black English, however, will have to work at changing their speech pattern later, when they want to operate within the larger social community. Similarly, children in some rural areas or in bilingual homes face a corresponding problem in working out later the refinements that make their speech more conforming to the generally accepted norm of society. Though English continues to change because of a variety of cultural influences, it is most unlikely that a major change in the direction of any particular dialect will occur. At best, English will add some words and expressions from dialects from time to time. If a reasonable norm of spoken English doesn't exist in the home, the parent will have to go ahead and surround the child with speech as best he can. It is better to do this than to risk the debilitating effect of verbal neglect of the child.

IT TAKES TIME

Though the quality of the speech model for the young child is of enormous importance, the *quantity* of speech opportunity—both for listening and speaking—is critical. Analytical attention to this matter in professional literature seems entirely lacking.

A neglected fact in learning to talk is the role of "overlearning." By overlearning is meant fixing in mind some fact or information through excessive repetition and use so that producing it when needed becomes completely automatic. That is, we reuse certain facts and information so much that their use becomes automatic on our part without effort to produce the intended response.

We overlearn our home address, telephone and social security number for example. Even years later, having moved to another city, we can still recall the old street number because it was overlearned at one time. Overlearning is most important to the young child who is acquiring a vocabulary, using parts of speech and developing a correct structural language. Each child learns the order of word use that is appropriate to his own language. In English-speaking homes the children soon learn the noun-verb-object sequence of the language. They also learn such things as forming the plural of nouns by adding *s* and indicating past-tense action by adding the suffix *ed* to regular verbs, or later that a different approach must be used for irregular verbs in English, as in the case of *see*, with its past-tense form *saw*.

Overlearning involves two processes. Either learners can greatly heighten their attention and concentration to the matter to be learned, or they can engage in a great amount of repetition, practicing the matter to be learned many times, or both. Each has its role in learning. For the young child learning speech, both processes are applicable, but repetition and practice seem to be predominant.

In the beginning, when the child is less than seven or eight months old, parents' language in the child's presence is quite general and without too much concern that words are to be learned. Just surrounding the child with talking to establish the general idea that conversation and oral language are natural seems enough. Even at the age of four months a baby will turn his head in the direction of human speech as evidence of being aware of it. Between the eighth and twelfth month the parent becomes more specific, intent and repetitious with certain words as a more conscious training effort in language for the infant. The parent is obviously working at developing language understanding by the child. Speech and language continue to fascinate children for many months.

In large part, the child at home learns his language by virtue of the time and repetition devoted to it. A startling fact is that between birth and age five years a child is exposed to language and is speaking or practicing speech for almost *twice* the number of hours that will be spent in formal schooling from kindergarten through grade six for *all* reasons for *all* subjects! This represents an enormous commitment of time to language while the young child is growing up. Aside from time spent sleeping, oral-language experience is the largest time allocation of the growing child.

Consider the total time the mother talks to the baby while feeding, bathing, diapering, and generally looking after the less-than-one-year-old. Note the time in the second six months of life devoted to babbling and the gradual shifting of intonation and pitch to more resemble human speech pattern.

It is estimated that at least six hours of the waking day for the one-year-old and up to ten hours of the waking day for the four-year-old are devoted to exposure to language or to the practice of language. These allocations over four years result in about seven thousand hours for *exposure* to language and another seven thousand hours for *practicing speech!* Assuming a maximum of six hours' instruction per day through the first six grades and about three hours' learning per day for the kindergarten year (each school year being 180 days), we have a total of slightly more than seven thousand hours. The enormous time allocation so critical for success in learning to speak and using English at home is a much underrated fact. In no way does it detract from the critical importance of the child's having a good speaking model, too. We shall return to these statistics in a later chapter dealing with learning to read.

The child himself initiates and carries out a significant portion of his own speech practice—first in babbling, then in solitary play, in asking an enormous number of questions, in group play with his peers, and through legitimate participation in the family conversational circle. The enlarging and conscious success the child is experiencing with language is a continuous and natural motivating force.

If the young disadvantaged neighborhood child, an institutionally raised child, and a neglected child are considered against the backdrop of the usual language exposure provided in most homes, it is easy to see how a cumulative language deficit can develop for them. Not only the enormous time factor, but other favorable conditions too, emphasize the importance of the home role. Language is the most prevalent learning activity of the preschool-age child and it will be involved in all of his other learning. Language is obviously needed to satisfy the small child's wants and can be used as a motivational lever by parents. Because the mother or some other adult is usually the continuing speech model and language stimulator for several years, reward reinforcement in various forms can be used effectively in the home.

Learning to speak is substantially accomplished by age four. The parent and the home exercise the most influential roles. A surprising amount of exposure and practice go into learning to talk. The development of speech is a continuous growth pattern from the first conscious attention to sounds of the human voice at about four months of age to basic mastery of speech skills and the elements of language structure at age four. The logical language need at that point is to begin the patient introduction of the *written* symbols of language for which the human brain, eye, ear and voice are ready.

3

The Remarkable Senses— Ready to Go

An oral vocabulary of several hundred words is necessary for beginning reading. A child who does not have such a vocabulary is not likely to be able to learn to read. A beginning reader must have prior knowledge of the oral meaning of the printed word he sees. The challenge is to attach the new visual form he sees to the oral meaning which is already part of his sound vocabulary. Without prior knowledge, the child has no mental meaning to associate with the printed symbols and thus cannot *read*.

As we have noted in an earlier chapter, the average four-year-old has a working vocabulary of at least 1,500 words. He can recognize hundreds more when he hears them. When he becomes six and enters school, he will encounter only about 350 different words in primers—roughly *one fifth of the number he knew two years earlier!*

If an oral vocabulary is essential to learning to read, the four-year-old is ready. He already knows hundreds of meanings. He can *decode* the oral sounds of words—that is, attach meanings to them. He is ready to learn how to decode printed words. It cannot be for want of a basic vocabulary that we delay learning to read until age six. Are other problems obstacles?

If a four-year-old's vision doesn't permit him to see printed letters or words clearly, he can't learn to read. If he can't hear sounds for letters or letter groups clearly, he won't be able to associate sounds with letter forms they represent. If his brain can't make the associations between sounds and letters and sounds and words, or if the effort would cause an undue mental strain, we should hesitate about starting reading. Since there is a natural enthusiasm for printing letters and words along with the excitement of learning to read, we need to know that muscular coordination in the hand is sufficiently developed. Finally, is teaching a child to read such a complicated procedure that only a professional teacher should attempt it? In short, regardless of the oral vocabulary of the child, there may be other reasons to keep him from learning to read at age four. Are there really?

PARALYZING PREJUDICES

As we learned earlier, educators have taken the position that a child who does not have a mental age of six or six and a half years is not ready to learn to read.[1,2] This position is based more on when children historically have been required to begin school attendance than on any serious determination of whether children can practically learn to read before age six. Actually, six is the age at which children traditionally first have been permitted to be away from home regularly for most of a day—at school! Compulsory school-attendance legislation is based on general social readiness of the child to be away from home rather than on educational and intellectual considerations.

Reading achievement has usually been judged starting at age six, with the typical methods and materials in use. Because of the failure rate found, some educators believe that teaching should be delayed even longer, until age seven or eight. It is time we looked at this educational history objectively and helped pre-school-age children learn to read earlier, when they are first ready. Children can learn to read before age six if parents help them. There is ample evidence supporting early reading.

A parallel educational example was our historic reluctance to teach foreign languages before the high-school level. It was assumed that only high-school students had sufficient maturity to learn another language. Until the myth was struck down by actually teaching foreign languages in junior high and elementary schools the belief continued. There are many successful foreign-language programs in elementary schools today. Internationally, where there has been a natural need to be bilingual, success in learning a second language has always been developed early.

If educators acted upon the evidence of their own research, they would not delay the teaching of reading until the first grade. A range of achievement by age and grade level is one of the clearest facts in education and one often ignored. The normal *range* in achievement at the first-grade level is between three and four years. That range means that when children in the first grade are tested, the results show some children can hardly read at all and others read as well as children do three grades higher in school. At the fourth-grade level the range is between five and six years.[3] Only two thirds of the pupils in a typical first-grade class have a mental age of six years. About 14 percent have the mental age of five, and another 14 percent score at age seven. Four percent are evenly divided between the mental ages of four and eight. These are the typical results from controlled testing of reading comprehension and language-related skills.

As schooling continues, the range in tested achievement among pupils gets larger. That is what we should expect. Very young children as an entire group are more alike mentally than they will ever be again. Education and experience over time result in greater and greater differences. The four-year range in mental age that characterizes first-graders steadily increases thereafter. A high-school teacher having a typical class of students must deal with a mental-age range of eight to ten years!

If we compare the *myth* about when a child should learn to read with the *actual range* of mental ages of children, we should be teaching some four-year-olds who have a true mental age of six years; and we should not be teaching some six-year-olds who have a mental age of only four years. However, mental age and going to school are not the point! This book will show that *all parents should teach basic reading skills to their four-year-olds who have an understandable vocabulary, because such children are ready.* The variation in mental ages among four-year-olds is less important than the fact that they usually have a large oral vocabulary and their sensory organs are ready to handle reading. These are the two main determinants of *when* the child is ready to learn basic reading skills—not when he can physically and emotionally go down the street or on a bus to school, or when state law compels it.

The popular prejudice about vision of preschool-age children says that they cannot handle the more exacting and disciplined task of seeing and working with letters and words. It holds that the effort to repeatedly focus on printed letters or words on a page will be harmful somehow and that a preschooler can't tell the difference between rather small things like a spider and an ant or between a paper clip and a safety pin—or between a *d* and a *b*.

The prejudice about vision claims that the muscles that control and direct the movement of the eyeball will become unduly tired if they are directed across too many lines of print. This prejudice stands on the assumption that full-blown reading tasks of several hours' duration will soon be attempted by (or be required of) children just learning to read. The vision task required in learning to read is quite different from sustained reading by a graduate student working all day in a library or an adult enjoying the latest novel. If a child's ability to focus on a word, or letter—or any small object—is limited, he may need a vision examination and eyeglasses or extra-large type at the outset. Common sense would call for the same corrective action regardless of the age of the subject or the nature of the fine-vision task to be accomplished.

Another prevalent prejudice is in regard to the ability of young children to hear sounds distinctly—a skill needed for associating sounds with their letter groups. Certainly, such letters as *e, b* and *c* sound somewhat alike, as do such words as *top, mop* and *pop*. But there are clear differences to be heard and learned. Ordinary four-year-olds already show their grasp of such differences in their speech. Directing their concentration to the matter of sound differences may require time, patience, repetition and praise, but parents will find that their child will learn to hear the differences.

Because children don't draw with the refinement of long-practiced older children or adults, there is a prejudice (by comparison) that they can't draw well enough to execute the forms of letters or copy words with sufficient precision. An examination of the actual copy work of four-year-olds who have had the benefit of some practice and encouragement will change the mind of all but the most biased.

The basic goal is to develop mental associations between letter and word forms and their names. If necessary, directed copy practice could be omitted and preprinted letters or letter blocks could be used. However, as will be shown later, the actual copy work is highly desirable. Some doubting adults might need practice and encouragement themselves, right now, to gain a reasonable control and produce creditable results in Japanese brush painting as a new skill. All first efforts with a new motor skill take practice and can be made more productive by a tolerant, encouraging coach. Children will be learning to read from prepared letters and words. Their own writing is reinforcing to their efforts and helps fix mentally their grasp of the forms involved. It does not serve as their word models.

Another prejudice to be overcome in creating a climate of confidence for the parent is the one that holds that the young mind and brain cannot handle the complexities of learning the printed code. How we learn to read or to decipher any code inside the brain is not understood. Our real knowledge has advanced little beyond identifying the structure and areas of the brain that serve as vision, hearing, speech, memory and motor-control centers. We are a long way from understanding how mental associations actually develop within the brain or how motor commands are sent out from the brain to require muscles of the larynx for speaking or those of the hand for writing to perform their tasks.

Only a small percentage of four-year-olds can be expected to have a brain deficiency or injury that would basically cause a problem in receiving nerve stimuli from the eye and the ear, and mentally building the associations involved in reading. It is more likely that delay until age six, well past the point of natural readiness to read, can introduce complications beyond those that might be present at age four. Once again, the interested parent has the best evidence in whether his child has gained a reasonable facility in speaking. The four-year-old who can talk understandably like most four-year-olds has demonstrated already the ability to make mental associations between what is heard and what is meant by it and to order the vocal muscles to say the words. There is little reason to believe that a comparable association and ordering ability will not be developed for what he hears *and sees* and what he says or writes, even though additional brain areas will be involved.

Finally there is the prejudice that says learning to read is such a complex process that only a skilled, professionally prepared teacher can carry out the task. The teaching profession itself fosters this view. Yet, the profession acts in quite a different manner in teacher-training programs.

More attention in teacher-training colleges is paid to how music or physical education is taught than how reading is taught. Only recently are some states getting serious about requiring new teachers to have some training in the teaching of reading before an elementary-teaching certificate will be issued. Many teachers still learn how to teach reading *after* they have a job and actually practice on first-graders for two or three years before they gain enough experience to avoid some of their earlier failures.

As recently as 1970, 40 percent of the states made *no requirement* of a new teacher to have any training in the teaching of reading before being licensed to serve in a school.[4] In few instances can a beginner in primary teaching claim to be really professionally prepared to teach a child to read.

The point here is not so much to censure the colleges and states as to emphasize that your child of six at school often will be learning to read at the hands of a person not professionally trained for that critical task. This is an unfortunate fact that compounds the evil of the unnecessary two-year wait before the child gets a chance at reading. This point is made to encourage parents to be confident that with some guidance—as provided in later chapters—and common sense, they can introduce their pre-school-age child to reading successfully at home.

If learning to talk suffered from the same prejudices that have plagued learning to read, many of us would hardly speak. There would be all kinds of myths and prejudices about how the child's vocal cords aren't ready or can't stand the voicing stresses that would be required; how the age-one ear is too immature to discriminate sounds in the necessary way; how the very young child's attention is too fleeting; how the parent doesn't know the ways to teach oral speech; et cetera. There would have arisen a long list of thou-shalt-not's about what words and sounds should be used first, if at all, et cetera.

Since parents *want* the child to learn to speak and have the expectation that he will learn, an enormous amount of time is devoted to care and reinforcement that lead the child into human speech. Why should that same successful parent accept a set of prejudices later at the very time when the child can talk openly and in detail with the parent about this new code of reading? In some ways learning to read is less awesome than learning to speak. Only if the proof, not the myth, is there, can we continue to impose a two-year wait on the child before he gets to read.

HEARING AND MEANING

The young brain, by age two, has amply demonstrated its re-markable capacity for making mental associations between ob-jects and names for them. How many times was the same word repeated before the nerve impulses for it finally registered in the brain as a "sound" that had arrived there before? Through repeti-tion, a gradual association between object seen and word heard began to form. By age four, the brain has assigned meanings to the sounds for hundreds of objects, people, actions, et cetera.

Learning to read, in principle, is a variation of the mental process already displayed in connecting objects with their sound names. In reading, the brain must receive nerve impulses from the eye and connect the printed word with its already mentally stored sound name as well as learning a new set of sounds for letters and letter combinations. A three-way association begins to form involving a printed name, the sound for which it stands, and the object, action, et cetera, that they both represent.

In speaking, the vocal cords are finally able to voluntarily reproduce a previously "banked" sound or word. With time and repetition, meanings for the words *chair, door, brother, dog,* and about fifteen hundred others have been grasped and stored mentally. Naturally, learning to read will require also a mental association for the individual sounds of letters and letter groups as well as whole words. The four-year-old's fifteen-hundred-word use vocabulary means that *eight to ten hours* of listening and speaking time, on the average, have been devoted to acquiring *each word!* This is a prodigious feat within the family. Though the very first word learned and uttered represents literally months of exposure to words, every day now, at four, adds new words to the child's vocabulary.

Remember the patience that was exercised and the importance of repetition and reinforcement in learning to speak? Fortunately, not so much time will be needed to develop a sight vocabulary of basic words or to learn the sounds for letters or letter groups, though at first it will be a slow process.

In the same way that very young children heard words and stored up sounds before the first whole word actually popped out, a similar process takes place when we begin to direct attention to the sounds that are associated with visual language symbols instead of the objects themselves. It was a long time before *doggie* and *ball* were voluntarily used in the child's vocabulary. He was shown his "doggie" and his "ball" many times, and the words were repeated many times in association with the objects before his brain made the actual connection between the sound and the object and correctly repeating the sound. We should expect again a process comparable to this mental "sound digestion" within the child—this time associating the sounds with visual letter symbols and words rather than with the real ball or the real dog alone. Now the child is faced with learning a series of word symbols that *stand for* the real thing.

Of course, it will take time. But think of the advantage you have in tackling the job now, since you and your child can talk to each other! When you first helped the child learn to speak, there was hardly any means of communication until the child's brain did its own grasping of the sense of the situation from all the surrounding sounds, gestures and actions.

HEARING AND READING

Hearing with reasonable accuracy is essential to learning to read. If a child can talk so that other people outside his family understand him, he has already demonstrated sufficient acuity to conclude that hearing should not be a problem for him in learning to read. If his speech is too immature or if he has not developed a fluent vocabulary, you should look into that matter first. If members of the family still use baby talk with the child or if he is playing with children who use baby talk frequently, he is not hearing the correct sound elements necessary for learning to read.

If, in spite of accurate adult-style speech around him, the child continues to speak in an unclear or infantile manner, a hearing impairment should be suspected. In this case, the question should be raised with the family physician or a clinic, and referral to a hearing specialist should be requested. Though the number of children with hearing problems is variously estimated, the figure of about 5 percent is frequently used. Many adults have had to live with permanent hearing difficulties that originated in childhood, one half of which could have been reversed if treated soon enough.[5]

It is not unusual for children with severe hearing losses to be classified as mentally retarded, emotionally disturbed or aphasic. The following common symptoms should alert parents to a possible hearing problem in their child: (a) greater awareness of movement than of sound; (b) frowning or strained expression when listening; (c) habitual inattentiveness; (d) inaccurate articulation; (e) turning of head in an effort to hear better; (f) confusion of words that sound alike; (g) interruption of conversation without awareness of others talking; and (h) draining or inflamed ear canals.[6]

The outer ear is only an appendage of skin and cartilage and serves little true function in hearing. The middle ear encloses a short tube that conducts the entering sound waves, which cause the eardrum at its inner end to vibrate. In turn, the vibrations set up a wave motion in the inner ear and thus stimulate tiny nerve cells. These cells join together to form the auditory nerves leading to the brain and carry nerve impulse energy for the original sounds. This miraculous system converts a great range and variety of sounds into nerve impulses. With practice, the hearing centers of the brain assign meaning to the impulses so that recurring sounds become understood and remembered.

Reading skill finally is dependent on being able to hear individual sounds that make up words—not just the words themselves. In a later chapter some sound practice suggestions are provided to help you decide whether your child needs a hearing examination.

Hearing is a vital part of living and learning. Hearing connects us with much of the world and our immediate environment. Given such a magnificent physical and mental system for hearing and assigning meanings to sounds, we should gladly accept the opportunity to help the young child learn the forty-four sounds of our language and the basic letter and word symbols that stand for them. He can and will—with your help.

SEEING LANGUAGE

Children must see words and letters clearly to learn to read. They cannot associate a sound or name with a letter or a word that they do not see clearly. Two questions must be asked about four-year-olds. Can they see well enough naturally for the reading task? And, if they can't, can limited vision be corrected for reading?

Four-year-olds exhibit an unusual ability to see, though they seldom have the task of discriminating between words and between letters. It is obvious from watching them that they carry out refined visual tasks. They discover and watch with fascination the antics of ants or the disciplined movements of a spinning spider. The young child can retrieve a small button or a thread, a paper clip or a dime dropped by a parent; can poke a shoe lace through its hole or put a pen into its holder; can point out the eyes of animals printed on pajamas, raindrops on a window pane or the set in a finger ring. In a hundred ways four-year-olds show that they have the visual acuity needed to clearly see letters of a size that would be intelligently used for beginning reading.

If seeing needs a little help, print size can be enlarged. Even as newspapers and magazines with larger type can be ordered now for older people with failing vision, we can be equally practical about what size of type will most help the four-year-old to see in learning to read. We did not hesitate to speak slowly or loudly or very distinctly, or to repeat, if it helped when we taught the child to talk.

The art of improving vision by using corrective eyeglasses is remarkably advanced. The extent of such handicaps among four-year-olds is not often noticed because they seldom perform fine visual tasks regularly under the supervision of their parents. Other adults are unlikely to notice a deficiency before the normal school years. Most four-year-olds should have an optometric examination, on general principles as well as to discover a possible obstacle to successful learning. Certainly, the examination is important; delaying it until after age six could saddle a child with a permanent impairment of vision.[7]

Visual acuity is the capacity to distinguish visual form and to note detail such as that involved in recognizing letters of the alphabet. This acuity requires that the optical apparatus of the eye itself function properly for image production; that adequate nerve stimulation be generated at the retina in the eye; and that meaning be assigned to nerve impulses when they reach the vision centers at the rear of the brain.

Most adults are aware of the expression "20/20 vision"—meaning normal vision. The expression comes from the original way in which visual acuity was tested. If a person standing 20 feet away from an eye chart can read on it the line of letters he should be able to read at that distance, he has 20/20 vision. If, for example, while standing at 20 feet, he can only make out the line of print that a person of normal vision can read at a 40-foot distance, his vision would be testing at 20/40 and he would need eyeglasses that would produce a 20/20 effect for him. Young children are tested the same way, except that, instead of reading letters they do not know yet, outlines of familiar objects are used as the vision target on the charts. It should be obvious that if the letters normally read from a farther distance were made larger, that difference could accomplish the same thing that eyeglass correction does. Practically, of course, this solution has its limits, since the real world uses for most printed messages a type size that is consistent with the size tested by a standard eye chart.

Problems in vision may be due to the shape or action of the eyeball or the various structures in it. A vision examination for a child normally includes near and far visual-acuity tests, a test for astigmatism, and a near-point convergence test. Aside from physical problems related to receiving and focusing light rays in the eye, a variety of disease conditions can affect the eye and vision. Parents with doubt about their child's vision should obtain for the child a total vision and eye examination.

There has been too little study of the vision of young children. An optometric symposium report states that the visual acuity of four-year-olds is estimated by experienced clinicians to be about 20/30.[8] This would mean a 91.5 percent visual efficiency for four-year-olds—good enough to handle comfortably the larger print used in children's books.

The common practice of using larger type in children's books is a practical recognition of this statistic and is a logical compensation for it. A parent using letters in teaching a child to read will use print at least one inch tall for the same reason. Larger print helps the child to locate the important differences in the forms of letters and words.

The same symposium reported unpublished data to show that only 4 to 6 percent of all four-year-olds fall below the 20/20 standard with best correction—that is, with eyeglasses—if needed.[9] Accordingly, good vision for beginning reading is either naturally present in this age group or can be readily attained through examination, diagnosis and the use of eyeglasses.

The intricacies of human vision are as impressive as the system by which we hear, if not more so. Though the mechanics of light entering the eye, being bent and focused take place within the eyeball itself, it is in the vision centers of the brain that *seeing* literally takes place.

Good vision depends on light coming to a perfect focus upon the retina of the eye. The point of focus depends on the changing shape of the lens within the eye, the curvature of the front of the eyeball, and the shape of the eyeball itself. If the eye cannot produce a naturally perfect focus, prescribed eyeglasses can make the focus fall properly upon the retina.

The six muscles that control the movements of each eyeball are among the most durable and tireless of the entire body. Only very prolonged fine visual tasks can pose a problem for them.

As in the case of the child's remarkable hearing system, his capacity to see is well developed. We cannot excuse ourselves in delaying reading on the grounds that the eye, the ear and the brain aren't ready yet. They are!

THE CHILD WRITING

Drawing letters and copying simple words is a natural and important part of learning to read. The act of forming a letter and copying a word is a personal achievement and is vitally reinforcing behavior in learning to read. A child who begins to recognize the forms of letters or a whole word (the child's name, for example) will want to print it. Printing and copying words should be viewed as strong supporting activities that promote better mastery of reading.

One of the first encouraging experiences of a child in forming a positive attitude about reading is copying words. Though copying at first will not mean knowing the letters or understanding the words, the child is experiencing the first heady sense of writing. In the next few months quite a few words will be learned from their general form and configuration without knowing their actual letter or phonetic composition. Even adults refer to the dictionary occasionally, because they too know the general form of a word but are unsure of its exact composition.

Printing letters and words helps to develop the concept of the interchangeability of letters in forming different words—a basic principle of our written code. Learning to read is aided by physically manipulating letters and words, including selecting and arranging letters that are printed on blocks or cards. Even experimentation with typewriters has been successfully employed with very young children wanting to express their creative desire to reproduce letters and form words.

A logical question arises. Can four-year-olds form letters and copy words well enough for personal printing to be a vital part of their activity in learning to read? The answer is yes. Printing, regardless of its crudity, is an important part of introducing your child to letters, their use in words and the system of writing. Reading (decoding) and writing (encoding) should be developed jointly whenever possible. They are mutually reinforcing activities.

We should not expect a preschool-age child to match adult standards in performing physical feats of skill. To learn to write is to learn a physical skill that will improve with practice and encouragement. If at one time we were tolerant of quite imperfect speech as we coached and urged the child to learn to speak more accurately, why should we expect this new skill of forming letters to emerge spontaneously? It will require its own time line for improvement and mastery. How many times did the child try to say "supermarket" before he could reliably produce the proper sounds in sequence each time he needed to use that word? He may have as much trouble in printing c-a-t for the first three dozen attempts, too, before some degree of readability is evident. Writing, like walking, speaking or riding a bicycle, is a learned muscle skill. To learn will take practice and will involve a large amount of trial and error before the pencil goes where it should. It will require a great deal of parental patience, praise and reinforcement of correct writing as it occurs (and an absence of criticism) if the skill is to be learned.

Though learning to read can proceed at first with less attention to the child's own forming of letters, eventual success and a grasp of the code system will be promoted by encouraging printing. Later chapters deal more exactly with this activity.

How much success can we expect a four-year-old to have in printing and copying words shown him? If he cannot hold and manipulate a pencil or pen reasonably well, we could be wasting time and seeking the impossible in trying to help him copy letters and words. Can he be expected to use the small muscles of his hand and wrist under his own conscious direction to accurately copy letters?

Using voluntary muscles and developing a progressive mastery over them has been the main daily activity of the average four-year-old for his entire life. Age four is a most energetic and active period. He attempts many, many things and particularly delights in executing feats of finer muscle control. He can cut along a line with scissors, lace his shoes, successfully stack a series of blocks on top of one another to make a tower, dress himself, button his clothes, brush his teeth, put small pellets into a bottle, trace patterns, and fold a paper several times in a prescribed manner.[10] In numerous ways the four-year-old demonstrates his control of fine muscles of the hand and wrist.

Young children have a natural instinct to be creative. Most parents are aware of how fascinated young children are with drawing and painting. They occupy themselves for hours with such activity. By age four, scribbling and aimless drawing that characterized earlier ages have disappeared in favor of more purposeful art and graphic expression. At four a greater sophistication in making more perfect circles with a clockwise motion is evident and a greater mastery in making straight lines is seen. This child can make a good cross with straight lines though he cannot draw some geometric forms, yet.[11]

A moment's reflection will remind us that the ability to make a circle and a straight line is the essential skill required to form any letter of the alphabet. The four-year-old has that skill.

Further observation of the four-year-old in drawing will show that he typically holds his writing instrument in a generally adult fashion—that is, with his thumb and the index and middle fingers. In fact, he acts to adjust the holding style with the opposite hand if necessary to "get ready" to draw (or write).[12] Thus we have the necessary skill present in the four-year-old to successfully copy letters and words. He naturally holds a pencil in a writing position. He can form circles and make a straight line. All that is needed is intelligent guidance and encouragement to bring forth reasonable facsimiles of our printed language.

The child's success in learning to form letters depends more upon his parent than upon himself. The ability to develop reasonable skill in printing already lies within the child. The parent, serving as coach and teacher, must show the same expectation and patience he displayed in teaching the child to talk. Remember, one year went by before even the first word was spoken and another ten months' effort were required to reach the hundred-word speaking level. Fortunately, learning the basics of reading and writing will proceed much more rapidly, and progress will appear in weeks. In principle, we are moving the child from free and casual drawing following his own moods into a more ordered and precise "drawing" of letters. The main point is that he is ready and able to successfully learn to execute more exact drawing, which will become printing in a few months. Though he may not know the names of all the letters he is forming when he is first copying, he will know that he is drawing a "picture" of a word. In time, he will acquire his own visual memory of the various letters and grasp the great idea of the interchangeability of letters to make new words.

Copying and printing are important reinforcing activities for reading. The four-year-old can hold a pencil well and can naturally make the essential strokes needed to copy or print. With practice and praise he will be successful in using these talents to become a better reader.

FACING THE FACTS

If a case is to be made for waiting until age six before beginning reading instruction, it would be made best on the grounds that the child's vision, hearing and thinking are too underdeveloped for the task. The claim would be that he cannot hear differences in the sounds of the language; that he cannot see the differences and distinguish between letters; and that he cannot make the mental associations necessary between words and letters and sounds they stand for. Further, if he could not copy or form letters and words he would be handicapped in writing, which has an important relation to learning to read.

None of these claims has been demonstrated to be true! Quite the opposite is actually true for four-year-olds. His own speech is the first strong evidence of good hearing. His naturally good vision, as well as the corrections made possible by eyeglasses, set aside the question of whether he can perform fine visual tasks. His mental ability to form associations has been exhibited first in learning to talk. His ability to make visual association with objects and events is well developed and can be carried over directly to words and their meanings. The durable eye muscles do not pose a real fatigue problem. He can make the basic marks needed to form letters, and he enjoys doing it. The four-year-old is physically and mentally equipped to learn how to read.

Aside from abilities native to the child himself, can we be optimistic about other possible problems? Classroom teachers are not that especially trained to teach reading, and they must try to teach the skill to two or three dozen children when they do. The interested parent in a one-to-one relationship at home has a substantial advantage if he will take some time to think about what it is he wants the child to learn each time they work on reading together. The parent must be willing to understand what needs to be done and why. He must be willing to exercise patience and praise in developing reading as he did in developing speaking earlier in the same child.

Finally, there is no special set of materials used in schools that are unique to teaching beginning reading that are not easily duplicated in the home at minimal cost or cannot be purchased at very modest cost.

We must conclude that there is really nothing about the four-year-old himself that makes learning to read impossible, or that justifies a continued delay until age six. For most children, *age four is the first age at which all the necessary prior experience and natural physical and mental conditions are present for learning to read successfully within a reasonable period of time.*

The dangers invited by imposing a two-year wait until age six are deserving of careful study and may demonstrate why some children and schools experience difficulty in the primary grades with reading. Eliminating the unnecessary two-year wait is a decision the parent must make. Denying the child the right to try as soon as he is really ready hardly seems possible in the face of the facts. Success will be almost unavoidable.

4

Reading
Four-Year-Olds

A theory should be only as good as the evidence that supports it. If a theory can be tested in a real-world situation, it should be. A theory may have to be accepted on the authority of acclaimed specialists until practical testing is possible. History, fortunately, is punctuated with examples of long-standing theories being overturned by a common-sense test or experiment.

The "flat-world" theory prevailed for a long time. It was not until the sixteenth century that Magellan's fleet, by sailing only westward from Spain, first proved the round nature of the earth by arriving back at their starting port.

A theory believed for centuries was that heavier objects fall at a faster rate than lighter objects. Galileo, by dropping two objects of different weight from the Leaning Tower of Pisa, proved that they reach the ground at the same moment.

A theory long held was that microbes and bacteria appear spontaneously in substances, and they do not have to come from other living forms. Pasteur, by sterilizing a substance, killing all organisms present and then protecting it from air and other contamination, proved that microbes cannot come into being spontaneously.

An unproven theory popularly believed for a long time is very difficult to overturn—even with facts. If such a theory is endorsed over a period of time by specialists, even in the face of contrary evidence, few will dispute it. An unproven theory can continue to affect the lives of people and even shape the culture before it finally collides with facts that refute it. The theory now widely believed that children must be six years old before they are able to learn to read successfully is unproven. It is time we recognize the contrary facts.

Child psychologists, physiologists and educator-philosophers have, all through this century, put forward unproven theories in such a way that they were established as unchallengeable law— that children must be six to learn to read. Maturational studies of children decades ago helped lock us into a view of fixed, sequential stages of child development. We were too willing to wait for a child to "grow out of" a phase or to "grow into" a new stage rather than believe we could do something to cause or uncover a greater readiness for certain behavior.

Physiologists warned that sensory organs and the nervous system *might* not be able to handle the requirements and discipline that reading *might* demand. Educator-philosophers were overly inclined to view childhood in an idyllic and maudlin sense and to believe that children should be left to mature "at their own pace" without worries and burdens of learning. Seldom did a researcher try to teach children younger than six to read, to see if the collective negative patchwork that produced this theory prevented reading success. However, some studies were conducted.

During the past fifteen years, the view of professionals has shown small signs of becoming less rigid. Even allowing for differences in definition of what reading means (and there are real differences among professionals), the attitude of the times is a little more open-minded and objective about this question. However, most of the emphasis of new inquiry is being directed to the early stimulation of young disadvantaged children rather than to the basic question of early reading for all preschool-age children. A few recent studies touch the question directly and promise to be part of a growing body of direct inquiry that will provide organized pragmatic evidence that young children can, do, and should learn to read long before age six.

Unfortunately, most studies on beginning reading will still be conducted in schools and institutions, where four-year-olds are not generally found. These studies will generalize about learning to read as a result of studying first-graders and kindergarten children instead of studying individual four-year-olds directly at home. The real need is for studies that reach into the home to observe the success of parents with individual children in teaching beginners to read. The in-home type of studies will continue to be neglected because the education profession starts from the premise that a teacher must do the teaching! Naturally, then, a study in which the parent does the teaching is excluded. It will be a long time before enough controlled studies have been completed to convince the average professional. However, there is nothing but fear itself about an unproven theory to prevent the parent from enjoying success in teaching his four-year-old to learn to read—at home.

It is time for parents to be their own Magellan, Galileo and Pasteur. It is time for you to go ahead and sensibly lead your child into reading and leave the explanations of how it happened to others later, if necessary. Fortunately, there are enough studies of success to make it unnecessary for parents to proceed blindly, irresponsibly or without help. The "children-can't-learn-to-read-before-they-are-six" theory must be refuted by parents who care enough about their child to go ahead and teach him to read.

FACTS ABOUT EARLY READERS

A few significant early-reading studies that have been made should convince any objective educator and all interested parents that four- and five-year-olds certainly can learn to read before they enter school. Some of these have been known for a long time.

Oakland and New York City

In recent years two studies have been especially concerned with children who learned to read before they entered school. One study in Oakland, California, began in 1958; the other, in

New York City, in 1961.[1] Both dealt primarily with children from blue-collar and lower-middle-class backgrounds.

In these studies, 205 children who had learned to read at home were identified at the start of their first-grade school year (49 in Oakland and 156 in New York). After identifying the children by means of a simple-vocabulary word list, each was given standardized reading tests. It was found, on the average, that they already could read at a level expected at the end of the first grade or at the start of the second grade.[2] The best of them were reading *at the fourth- and fifth-grade levels* when they entered first grade. They had not learned to read in kindergarten. They had learned at home!

These children came from homes in which the parents were interested in their development and were responsive to their interest in printed language. In Oakland, 86 percent of the identified pupils were from lower-middle-class families or below. In New York, the pupils came from a heterogeneous population in Manhattan, Queens, Brooklyn and the Bronx representing a rather even socioeconomic distribution, including Spanish-speaking Puerto Rican children. The intelligence of the identified children showed a wide range—91 to 161 I.Q. in Oakland and 82 to 170 I.Q. in New York. The median of each group was high (122 in Oakland and 133 in New York).

Even the least able of the children read as though they had already completed four or five months of the first grade. The range of tested achievement by grade-level norms was 1.5 to 4.6 in California and 1.4 to 5.2 in New York. The median grade-norm scores (the point above and below which one-half of each group scored) was 1.9 in Oakland and 2.0 in New York City.[3]

It is not unusual in first-grade classes to find a pupil who has already learned to read. This fact led to the effort in these studies to locate a group of such children for testing and further analysis of the factors that had contributed to their early start. These studies were aimed also at determining how well the early-reading advantage would continue in later schooling.

The 205 children were located by using a list of all words that were common to the preprimers of the three basal reader series most frequently used in the Oakland schools. In all, a list of 37 words was obtained (see Table 1). In addition, several of the words were also shown as sentences to promote recognition from context—a subskill in reading.[4] Children who could recognize and say orally at least half the words on the list were arbitrarily identified as "early readers" for the purpose of the study. They had learned to read, in this sense at least, before they entered first grade.

Though these studies were begun primarily to trace the continued reading progress of the children through the elementary grades, our emphasis here is on the demonstrated fact of reading skill that they had acquired at home before instruction at school. These children had already learned the initial target vocabulary of beginning reading before they came to school. Obviously, for these children, the initial teaching of reading had taken place at home.

The end results of the studies in Oakland showed that early

TABLE 1

Durkin Early Reader Word List Screen (Oakland, California)

said	to	down	jump
mother	for	big	house
red	it	in	blue
want	father	here	we
can	is	work	away
help	stop	little	ball
get	and	funny	you
the	come	play	see
look	make	me	go
			not

The ball is red.
Come and look.
Come and see the ball.
It is not big.
It is little and red.
Mother said it is for me.

readers continued to hold an advantage over their non-early-reading classmates as they proceeded through the next six grades. This finding is contrary to the popular theory that early-reading children will encounter problems, suffer boredom and experience a subsequent loss in achievement.

In New York, the longitudinal phase of the study was continued for only three years. At the end of that period, the children's achievement, on the average, was even higher than that of the Oakland early-reading group at the same stage of school.

Denver

Historically, reading has been taught to first-graders at age six as the logical first skill to be developed. As attendance in kindergartens by age-five pupils increased (over 60 percent of that age group now attend kindergarten nationally), we might have expected that significant experimentation in the teaching of reading to this age group would be carried out. Even with five-year-olds so conveniently at hand, educators have refrained from either offering the opportunity or constructively experimenting with planned reading instruction for them. The collective prejudice and the national tradition against such instruction for "below-sixers" have paralyzed our initiative.

The role of the kindergarten usually has been restricted to a variety of general "readiness" activities pointing toward "real" schooling in the first grade. The educational objectives of kindergartens have been expressed traditionally in terms like "building feelings of adequacy"; "giving the child opportunities to explore and understand his world"; "facilitating growth through providing space, freedom and equipment needed"; "helping him find a contributing place in the group . . ." et cetera.[5] A specific and tangible objective such as developing basic reading skills is foreign to the kindergarten experience in most schools, though a few teachers and boards of education take steps in that direction.

A parent, knowing the true nature of his five-year-old, would expect, on the basis of the natural readiness and ability of the child, that kindergarten would be a fertile ground in which reading could take root. However, kindergartens, at best, in their two-hour-plus day may encourage improved listening skill or visual recognition of a few words posted about the room. The teaching of beginning reading as one of their goals is avoided.

A significant study of the teaching of reading to kindergartners, though, was begun in Denver, Colorado, public schools in 1960. The object was to teach the pupils to read, and to follow their progress on through the fifth grade.[6] In the study approximately four thousand pupils in kindergarten were randomly assigned to four types of control and experimental groups. Each experimental group received twenty minutes of reading instruction daily.

Seven teaching activities were provided to promote beginning-reading ability: using only context for supplying a likely word; listening for beginning consonant sounds; distinguishing letters from one another; using context and the beginning consonant sound; associating letter sound and forms; using context and the beginning letter; and using context and the strange printed word. These activities were especially planned for kindergarten pupils and were intended as an early sequential development of certain skills basic to learning to read. The same plan was used with some first-grade groups, also.

When the kindergartners who had been taught by the early-reading plan were tested at the end of their first-grade year of school and their reading achievement was compared with that of first-graders taught the same way but only for their first-grade year, the kindergarten-trained groups had significantly higher achievement in reading.

The superiority of the groups whose early reading training began in kindergarten was maintained over a period of several years in both vocabulary and comprehension. In the years following kindergarten, when the teacher at each new grade level made practical adjustments in the curriculum to capitalize upon the reading levels of the early-trained children, the pupils showed maximum achievement. Further, children who had been taught to read in kindergarten and who had received a continually adjusted reading program later, tended to perform better in other school subjects which involved reading, such as social studies, language, arithmetic concepts and some science. In the summary of the Denver study, the investigators made special note of the fact that the serious provision of reading instruction in kindergarten did not cause reading disabilities later in school.[7]

The broad applicability of the methods and the findings from this large public school district's study emphasized that "most average youngsters in a large-city public-school system can profit from beginning reading in kindergarten."[8]

The Denver study is clear testimony that when five-year-olds in kindergarten are provided with a planned beginning-reading program they make definite progress even with only twenty minutes' daily instruction. It is important to note that this study included all types of kindergartners. The study is strong evidence that we have been neglecting instruction in beginning reading, even when the children were at school under the supervision and guidance of teachers. It stands as silent testimony that if all children were required, by law, to attend school at age five, we would probably be teaching them to read at that age—successfully.

Palo Alto, California

Under the supervision of Stanford University's Department of Psychology, an important study in early reading was conducted more than forty years ago. This study was aimed particularly at beginning-reading achievement of children having a *mental age of four years,* though their chronological ages were three, four and five years. The subjects studied were bright three-year-olds, typical four-year-olds and dull five-year-olds. All had the mental age of four years. Specifically, the experiment was directed at finding out to what extent children with that mental age could learn to read, and whether bright, average and dull children, all with the same mental age, would learn to read equally well under the same conditions.[9]

The experimental study involved only thirteen children, with at least four in each group, under carefully controlled conditions. Each group met over a four-and-a-half-month instructional period. The instruction involved an individual ten-minute daily reading lesson and a brief group game related to reading. The instruction was begun after twelve days of general preliminary kindergarten-type activities and games. No child experienced more than sixty-one reading lessons.

One measure of reading achievement for the groups was their ability to recognize words out of context. At the close of the experiment, on the average, the bright three-year-olds recognized 129 words; the four-year-olds recognized 55 words; and the dull five-year-olds recognized 40 words. The range in recognized words among all the children was from a low of 20 to a high of 269 words. Based on the time allocated for instruction, this achievement was developed after *only ten hours of accumulative individual instruction time* (plus comparable group game time). The over-all calendar time involved, four and a half months, was less than the time normally devoted to a single school semester. The average achievement of the three-year-olds in this period exceeded that expected at the end of the first semester of the first grade.[10] The two best pupils scored at a level to be expected at the end of the first grade.

Though the study showed clearly that brighter, younger children will achieve more in reading than duller, older children, all with the same mental age, the study demonstrated reading progress for *all the children* even in such a relatively short time. The materials used in the experiment included a graded series of "massed forms" (that is, block outlines of different whole-word shapes); flash cards with words in half-inch print; charts with printed stories; a reading rack in which various words could be placed and rearranged to form simple sentences; and a variety of usual kindergarten materials such as crayons, scissors and blocks.

Ability to read was defined as the ability to associate a word name with its printed symbol; ability to discriminate between printed symbols; and ability to derive meaning from printed symbols.

Other important conclusions from the Palo Alto study were (1) that stimulating home environment had helped the bright three-year-olds; (2) that early training in reading had no harmful effect on the children, but actually increased their interest in books and stories; (3) that usual reading teaching in the first grade seems to take an unnecessary amount of time; and (4) that excellent eye habits for reading can be established at age three and a half.

Though the advantage of precociousness (in the bright three-year-olds) is indicated by the results of this study, the clear fact of reading achievement by dull preschool-age children is also demonstrated! Above all, the fact of children with a mental age of four years making substantial progress in reading in a relatively short time is strongly shown.

Mass Media Applications

If *parents* of preschool-age children are to be reached across the nation to orient them to methods and materials that can be helpful in developing early reading skills, it will be necessary to use wisely the medium of television and newspapers. Fortunately, some experimental efforts have already been carried out. It is unlikely that preschoolers can be taught to read directly through open broadcast television.

In Denver, following the successful launching of the public school's kindergarten reading program, the local educational television station offered preschool reading instruction to all interested viewing parents. To assess the results, three particular groups of parents were selected. One group served as a control without changing the usual home routines. A second group received a special guidebook called *Preparing Your Child for Reading*, to upgrade their ability to teach reading skills to their children. A third group also received the guidebook and, in addition, met with teachers in small discussion groups using films of the sixteen television broadcasts. The children of the three groups were tested before and after the broadcast series.

The use of television, personal orientation and the guidebooks were the most effective techniques. The experiment showed (1) that a preschool child with a mental age of at least four and a half years can be taught some beginning-reading skills at home by parents; (2) that the amount learned is related to the amount of time someone practices the reading skills with the child at home (at least thirty minutes a week are necessary); (3) that the parent who just reads regularly to his child can produce a measured change in reading achievement; and (4) that the best results come from instruction for at least thirty minutes a week with the parent reading to the child for at least sixty minutes a week. Eighty percent of the parents thought that the instruction they received was helpful and was important for their children. Three fourths of the parents wanted more help.

In 1964, the *Chicago Tribune* embarked on a plan to assist interested parents in teaching preschool children elements of reading. The newspaper published a series of 91 cartoon strips designed around simple phonetic explanations. The response from readers was of such a large volume and continued for so long that the newspaper repeated the series in 1969. Though no control measure was employed, the highly complimentary letters from thousands of parents testified to its value.

Other television stations and newspapers have engaged in a variety of plans to offer help to parents and direct stimulation to children.

Rome, Italy

The work of Dr. Maria Montessori in developing language skills in young children has a direct bearing on our view of four-year-olds. She conducted writing and reading experiments with young children assembled from tenement homes in Rome early in this century. Her work and conclusions are a significant study. Though, of course, the language involved was Italian, which is more phonetically consistent between sound and letter than English, the principles of Montessori's work have applicability for English.

Dr. Montessori, a physician, after early work in a psychiatric clinic, experimented in educating defective children in Rome. She had substantial success. The children learned to read and write, and they passed the usual examination in those skills for normal children in the public schools. As a result of her work, she was puzzled about why the usual procedures in schools were so unproductive. Because of her success and interest, she was invited to organize and direct a proposed series of infant schools to serve tenement areas in Rome. She opened the first school in 1907 gathering together fifty of the least promising children ages three to six.

The educational thinking of the time held that a child of eight years was barely equipped for the difficult process of learning to read and write and that attempting the alphabet for normal children at age six was questionable. In retrospect she expressed the view that "I was a victim of the prejudice that the teaching of reading and writing should be put off as long as possible and should not be introduced before a child was at least six."[11]

The hopes and interest of the parents, and Dr. Montessori's own earlier success with defective children, led her to begin instruction in reading and writing in the new school. Strongly convinced that writing was the easier of the two processes, she began at that point with her two assisting teachers.

The plan included learning to hold a pencil correctly, to pass it lightly over a surface and to guide the hand movement. Thereafter, the child traced geometric outlines using a form for that purpose and concentrated on coloring the form carefully.

To develop a better physical and sensory impression of letters the child touched and traced with a finger the form and shape of individual letters which had been surfaced with a fine sandpaper and were attached to a larger card. The child at four delighted in this exercise, saying the sound of the letter in the process. The sounds, not names, of letters were taught. From these sensations of sight, sound and touch, and with practice, the child soon became able to select any letter on request.

As soon as the child could recognize some of the vowels and consonants, he began to compose words using them. Montessori recorded that the child of four is very enthusiastic in the process, while the child at five shows a decline in the sensitivity and creative attitude most needed. She described how such basic preparation with letters and sensorimotor experiences leads to a veritable explosion in writing by the child. The elapsed time from the first attempt to perform the preparatory exercises to the first written word for the four-year-old child is one month and a half.[12] The five-year-old requires a month. In general, the children become proficient in three months' time.

Montessori's definition of reading was the interpretation of an idea by means of graphic symbols. At a minimum, the child who knows the meaning of a word that he has formed from movable letters but that has not been said to him, really reads.[13]

Dr. Montessori emphasized, as a first step in reading, the recognition of the names of known objects. These were usually in the room, were brought in or were well-known items. She and her teachers prepared hundreds of cards showing well-known words. The child would slowly translate the printed word into letter sounds and say the sounds more quickly to "hear" the whole word already in his speaking vocabulary.

As to the over-all length of time needed for a child to learn to read, Montessori reported, "Experience has shown us that, beginning from the moment when a child writes, it takes an average of about fifteen days to pass from the lower form of activity, writing, to the higher form, reading."[14] She further observed in speaking about later applications of her methods, "Almost all normal children who have been trained according to our methods began to write at four, and at five they can read and write at least as well as children who finished the first grade."[15]

When we remember the unpromising group of preschoolers from tenement homes who were the pupils, Dr. Montessori's results are, indeed, impressive.

Individual Experiences

Most children show some ability to recognize letters and words before they start to school, regardless of whether anyone has really worked with them on such a skill or not. It is a rare child who rides in the family car who doesn't learn and take pride in knowing the word *STOP*, when he sees it on a traffic sign. Television commercials and other advertising media have made many words common to preschoolers. Dozens of examples make it clear that repeated visual presentation of words to young children results in their learning to recognize the words and announcing them with pleasure.

Most children are asking about letters and words long before they enter kindergarten. It is the interest shown by parents in nurturing and responding to such questions that determines largely when the child will begin to read. Without response from adults and without direct encouragement, the child's real start in reading will have to wait until he is in school. With interest and help at home there is little question that reading ability can be developed, without strain, before the child is enrolled in school.

Reading interest is activated in many ways for preschoolers. Older children already in school, and playing school with a younger brother or sister, can provide a powerful reading stimulus. A parent is usually the main motivator. Just having books and words around the house can be the trigger. A few children will almost work out the reading code themselves if reading materials are easily at hand. A parent with a conscious but unpressured plan is most likely to develop reading skill in the preschool child. He has the special advantage of prolonged association with the child and exclusive attention in developing reading as the goal.

Several accounts are recorded of parents devoting time especially to develop reading skills in their young children. One, of
special interest and well documented, is that of Karl Witte.[16]

Karl was the son of a minister in the town of Lochau, Germany. Pastor Witte was doubtful about the quality of education
his young son would receive from the local schoolmaster and
determined to provide instruction himself. When Karl was very
young, his father initiated a plan of education that included, in
part, instruction in learning to read and write. Pastor Witte's
teaching, though it is exceptional in its concentration, dramatizes
the parents' opportunity to manage the environment of their
child to obtain positive educational results.

When Karl was very young, his father and mother began
showing him pictures and etchings, and telling him stories about
them. They took him on walks and generally talked about objects
in nature and the environment. After discussing some picture
books with Karl, his parents would conclude with the wistful
expression, "Oh, if you only knew how to read! It is a most
interesting story, but I have no time to tell it to you now." This
and other parental behavior were calculated to heighten Karl's
interest in printed words.

While Karl was three, he began to express interest in the
printed stories. His father purchased several sets of letters of the
alphabet. The letters were cut from wood and were three inches
high. They were placed in a box and drawn out blindly as a game
for Karl and his parents on the floor. In these fifteen-minute-a-
day games the parents examined and admired each letter, to fix
attention on it, and showed it to Karl while firmly saying its
name. The letter was handed around in turn among the three and
was named again. Whenever Karl said the name correctly, he
was praised and fondled. Mistakes were passed over lightly,
sometimes with a small chiding.

The parents controlled the mix of the letters in the box and
arranged for the vowels used in every word to be drawn out
more often in the early weeks of the game to increase practice
with them. As a result of this "game," Karl acquired mastery of

all the letters in several weeks and moved on to forming syllables with their sounds and then words. When Karl was four, he was forming sentences based on his quarter-hour-a-day regimen. Finally, Karl's reading skill was well-enough advanced to warrant the purchase of books more appropriate to his skill.

An analysis of Karl Witte's experience highlights the importance of several factors: (1) the conviction and expectation of parents that their efforts will be successful; (2) the value of regular but brief planned exposures to language, using pictures and local area trips as stimuli; (3) the introduction of letters when the child expresses a natural interest in them, including emphasizing the functional vowels early; (4) the value of pre-formed letters that can be handled; (5) the concept of the combination and interchangeability of letters; (6) the arrangement of words into sentences; and (7) providing praise and approval for correct responses and generally passing over errors.

The account of Karl is presented only to illustrate the impact that is possible from regular effort and interest of parents. Karl's experience, in fact, is quite unusual. Even though his father insisted that the lad was not particularly precocious, he provided him with a broad educational program. As a result, when Karl was nine he had learned five languages. At the age of fourteen he was certified for a doctorate at the University of Leipzig.

Those who are tempted to read too much precociousness into the Karl Witte account should be reminded that dull five-year-olds and bright three-year-olds learned the basics of word recognition and reading from only twenty minutes' daily exposure as previously described.

A number of individual accounts have been printed describing the success of parents in personally tutoring their young children of preschool age. Invariably success with language and reading are emphasized, though accounts report success in science, mathematics and other fields as well. Each is a tribute to the interest and patience of the parent and the inherent ability of the young child.

READING-FAVORABLE HOMES

Since the facts show that a wide range of three-, four- and five-year-olds, alone, a few together or in a group, having below average, average and high I.Q.'s, from working-, middle- and upper-class families, in all parts of the nation and in other countries, under different modes of instruction (sometimes by professionals with a plan and other times by parents without a plan), learn to read, *we must conclude that children have this potential before they go to school.* If the prevailing maturational theory of child development were valid, such a plethora of successful early readers could not be possible. Yet, they have learned to read.

The studies, experiments and reports presented in the previous pages lead to only one conclusion: children with a mental age of four years can learn to read. They should be given the opportunity.

A child has reached the point at which he can successfully go ahead with specific instruction about words, letters, names and their sounds, when he begins to ask questions about words and print. Until that point is reached, the parent should provide an environment that will bring the child and words together. The simplest act is to continue reading stories to the child regularly in a pleasant manner.

When a child signals his beginning interest and curiosity about print by exclaiming, "Show me my name," "What does the word say?" "What is that letter?" and so forth, he is ready to begin short periods of specific daily orientation and instruction in basic reading. His rate of learning to read can be dramatically accelerated over the next few months by earnest attention to his questions. When the child is interested, the parent should act. The youngster's questions are a clear sign that he has arrived at his "teachable moment" for beginning reading. To ignore this moment imposes an unfair burden on the child later, when he will be introduced less naturally to reading.

The questions of the four-year-old about words and letters

show that he is standing at the "reading gate" and that it can be opened by his parents. Without help, the gate will remain closed to him for many months. If it is opened by the parent, the child will pass through into a new and exhilarating experience with his language.

What are the conditions that are more often present in homes where four-year-olds have learned to read? Children generally first become aware of words and letters as a result of parents taking time to read stories to them. This activity over several months develops a consciousness that those marks on the pages say something about the pictures. The repetition of favorite stories from familiar books begins to establish the notion that the marks must always say the same thing because the pages get turned at the same stage of the story each time. The child's grasp of this notion is established when he begins to tell the parent when it is time to turn the page or he begins to turn the page himself, knowing from memory, finally, when all the words are through on that page. Naturally, it is important to read the story so that the child can easily see the pictures and the words.

Homes of preschoolers who learn to read usually include adults who themselves regularly read and serve as models. One or both parents in the home of most reading preschoolers read more than the average adult. If there are older, school-going brothers or sisters who have some homework reading to do, or otherwise enjoy the skill, the preschooler sees their example of using books and writing. The utility and pleasure from the process are self-evident in the home. The child develops an expectation and desire that he, too, is going to read and write. Knowing that others in the family read makes it natural and easy for him to ask questions about words and letters and to expect to receive help.

Though better-educated parents tend to provide more reading materials in the home and tend to read more themselves, they sometimes do not act to help their preschooler learn to read. Curiously, this is because they are more aware of the school's attitude about parents keeping a "hands off" relation to beginning reading. This is unfortunate, but it will change in the present decade. Parents less in touch with the school are less alert to contemporary school philosophy, and they may be inclined to go ahead and help their preschooler with words and letters believing they are helping to assure a greater first-grade success for him later—which they are.

Older brothers or sisters already in school often delight in playing school at home, using the younger child for a pupil while they act as teacher. Reading-related activity is a very natural subject for such play. The experience is mutually beneficial. At the least, it adds some positive experience of words and letters to that which a parent may provide for a beginning reader.

Preschoolers who scribble and have plenty of crayons, paper, felt pens, etcetera, tend to develop a stronger interest in copying words and letters than do children starved for the materials of such personal creative expression. By age four, scribbling as a natural activity has stopped and more organized drawing or copying has begun. Copying letters and words is an easily stimulated activity—and a fascinating one for most children. Parents wanting to help their child to learn to read should make plenty of drawing, copying and writing materials available.

The preschooler tends to "soak up" the positive reading environment that surrounds him. Unless words, letters, books, paper, pencils, and people reading are a part of the daily environment, the child has little opportunity to become oriented to the naturalness of reading, the frequency and value of words and their role in daily life.

Television is a natural part of a child's world and affects him. To balance the influence of general television in the life of the child, parents must also provide varied reading materials that will affect his development. The child cannot ignore either influence. Unless a word environment is created, the child cannot respond or get interested in printed language and reading. Though television and TV commercials can help to create an interest in words, by far the greater interest is stimulated by parents through other kinds of activities.

A preschooler who learns to read is often persistent in pursuing his interests. For instance, he will copy words or numbers or letters day after day in a very repetitious but personally satisfying way and then turn to another activity in a series of plateaus of interest. Copying at his own pace seems self-reinforcing. Growing mastery breeds more practice. The role of the parent is to answer questions, to provide materials and to offer correct models when it is helpful, without requiring exact performance or pressuring for too particular a style of execution.

It is wise to provide, along with writing materials, a blackboard that can be erased and used over and over or changed with less effort than that needed for pencil erasures. A small slate for the child's lap and a larger blackboard mounted at a height that the preschooler can reach can be important tools for reading progress.

By age four, the child's parent should be providing a good balance between toys, games and play equipment on the one hand, and books, letter blocks or cutouts, blackboard, crayons and diversified reading materials on the other hand. Even as the presence of television and the absence of books and magazines diverts inordinate time of adults to watching television, so can too many active toys and games and the absence of reading materials keep the young child from developing a natural interest in language and learning to read.

A positive force for encouraging reading by preschoolers is a parent who capitalizes on the natural presence of words in many places during the normal day with the child. In the kitchen, Mother can make a somewhat exaggerated process out of checking the wording on cans, cartons and containers for instructions, contents, et cetera, to help establish with the child that those marks are words and tell what is inside and what should be done with the contents. The child can find name labels he knows at the store to "help" with the shopping. The cookbook recipe tells an interesting story itself, and the child begins to note the different functions of words in his parents' world.

Short walks, or trips on the bus or in the car provide a multitude of words all around to talk about. Most parents see the child's exhilaration in his first recognition of words like "Stop," "Milk," "Ice Cream," "School Zone," etcetera. The world of the preschooler is literally drenched with words.

Why wouldn't any normal four-year-old develop a great curiosity about words and a desire to read like everybody else? His already-developed speech and a sense of grammar give him a built-in desire to see in another form the same words he knows ("Show me my name," et cetera). To deny a four-year-old the opportunity to pursue this interest and begin to learn how to read during the two years before he enters first grade is unnatural for a parent who normally is interested in his child, and it is an unwarranted thwarting of the mental and social nature of the child.

5

Why Not
Just Wait?

"Just because a four-year-old can learn to read, doesn't mean he should be taught." That is the last-gasp position of those who reluctantly admit that the child can be taught to read, but really feel emotionally that he shouldn't be. A lot of things in this world could be done, but should they? The answer, in general, must stand on the benefits to be gained, the cost in time, effort and dollars to do the deed, and whether it is realistic to attempt the proposed feat. How do these factors square with teaching your four-year-old? It will require modest but regular investment of your time; the dollar cost will be negligible, and it is realistic to go ahead.

We are not talking about some strange and exotic behavior or an interesting trick to be seen on television or some cute exhibition for the neighbors. We are not talking about getting your child to do something that will permit you to have a new set of ego-feelings about how intelligent you must be if your child can learn that kind of thing. We are talking about the most important of all human skills—the ability to manipulate language. We are talking about a skill your child will continue to develop and refine intensively over the next ten years and indefinitely thereafter.

Learning to read is not accomplished in a fixed period of time. It is not a new skill learned in just the first grade—or the second or the third. It is a skill having a very slow general beginning, a rush of concentrated progress and a very long and continuing refinement over several years.

WHY BOTHER A FOUR-YEAR-OLD?

Our view of your child learning to read must be based on two matters—understanding the child and understanding the process of reading. Once it is clear that the child's native ability permits him to learn to read, a clear choice exists as to when the skill should be developed. There must be an optimal time. The optimal time *for society* historically has been when children could be grouped together in schools with paid teachers to do the job. The optimal time *for the child,* though, usually is at age four, before he goes to school. There is reason to believe, too, that the best place for beginning is in the home rather than in a school.

It is quite apparent that four-year-olds can learn to read. Since they are not compelled by law to be in school, the decision on whether they shall learn to read early remains with the parent. A parent, interested in earlier-than-first-grade reading for his child, may hope to place the responsibility upon some institution such as a nursery school or hope that a public kindergarten will seriously start the job. These are false hopes and will be commented on later.

Naturally, you are concerned about whether you will be able to really do an adequate job with your child. Not only can the typical four-year-old learn to read, but his parent, in most cases, can teach him successfully.

In making your decision about this matter you face a dilemma. On the one hand, you see the opportunity to develop much earlier than usual a basic skill that your child will use all of his life and that will be fundamental to his whole school progress later. On the other hand, out of your lack of precise information, you have self-doubts about whether you will really understand and do it right. You don't want to cause a problem for the child later.

To improve the ability of a child to communicate is never a wrong decision. The thought never crossed your mind that you shouldn't work at teaching him to talk. In fact, you were so eager to get on with that job that you spent a lot time on it very early, with no idea of whether it was having any effect. You were completely confident of the coming need for your child to talk. You knew that he would be in contact with his environment more effectively when he could talk. You knew that there were many things about living in the home, being at play and around the neighborhood that made talking an attractive and essential skill. The child's ability to learn generally was enormously accelerated when he did learn to talk.

Childhood wouldn't be much fun if a child couldn't talk. Much of life is talking. The work of the world depends on talking, and so does satisfying play—both for children and for adults. It would be no favor to the child not to teach him to talk. Teaching him to read stands on parallel principles.

Maturational theorists and those who believe that childhood should be left alone to run its course finally concede that a time does come when childhood must be put away and other matters of the world take precedence. Their image of childhood is unduly colored with visions of the carefree child in the park, by the brook, lying on his back in the grass, a smile on his face; or the child is seen running through a field with the wind in his hair and a dog alongside. They break the world into the fun of being a child and the necessity of going to school and facing the world. They have trouble in reconciling pleasures of the physical world and exhilarations of the mind. They equate freedom from responsibility with happiness. They believe that childhood should be a scooping-up of good times and happy memories against the dread days to come. They cannot accept the unfolding of life at all ages and the progressive relating of the human organism to all of its environment. They do not understand that the human mind wants, seeks and *must have* a continuing flow of mental stimuli. A prolonged diet of "pleasure experiences" is as unnourishing emotionally and mentally as is a chronic diet of rice physically.

What does a young child do if he learns to swim before he goes to school? He swims sometimes and enjoys it, and thereby becomes a better swimmer. What does he do if he learns to skate at age four? He skates as opportunities permit, and he enjoys it. Any of the skills the young child acquires he uses and enjoys, and he improves them with practice. His early pleasure in the skill may be colored by the way he was taught. Nonetheless, he will enjoy exercising it. A skill acquired is to be used as circumstances permit or require. A person who enjoys a new skill will seek out ways to use it. So it will be with reading.

If a child can sing, he sings. If he can draw, he draws. If he can skate, he skates. If he can read, he reads. Reading, though, is a skill more integrated with life. It is involved with the daily world for a lifetime. It is much more than an occasional recreational skill. It is the stuff of living.

Since every parent expects his child to learn to read sooner or later, it should be an advantage to learn earlier. Is it? It has long been observed that the children most likely to finish first grade as the happier, better readers are those who started the school year knowing many of their letters and sounds. The Denver study cited earlier showed that children who learn to read starting in kindergarten did better in later grades in reading and language as well as in other subjects which lean heavily on that skill. Some older studies report that children who started to read in first grade catch up in later grades with those who started early. This phenomenon, where it occurs, can be laid more to teachers imposing a routine, uninspired reading program on the early trained readers and effectively denying them the chance to continue to improve their skills with appropriate instruction and materials than to any flash-in-the-pan performance from early training. Those who argue this catch-up line also think that it is only how well you finally read as a technical process at grade five that is important—not whether learning to read was a pleasant experience or whether the advantage of enjoying and using the skill for an extra year or two was good or whether the child benefited from what he read while he waited for the first-grade year to arrive. Their fixation is that it is a race and that the measure is degree of reading excellence at grade five or six. Any early reader's enthusiasm and progress at school can be dampened by ordinary instruction or enhanced by alert and competent teaching.

Maturationalists think they are arguing for acquiring reading naturally and without stress. They discount the enforced waiting period with its frustration for the four- and five-year-olds. True maturation—that is, readiness for reading—is at age four. That is when it is natural and least stressful to learn the language symbols. The maturationalists feel that the percentage of nonreaders and reading failures arising at first grade is an inevitable price, and they refer only to those who do learn to read. They can't entertain the possibility that many reading failures might be avoided altogether by early natural starting in the home.

In our world of words, it is becoming increasingly clear that children are frustrated by having to wait to learn to read until they can enter school in the first grade. Frustration should be expected, considering how the children are reminded every day of their nonreader status. At four you have the child's genuine attention, and he is asking the right questions that permit reading to get started naturally. For the child, it is a simple question being answered, at first. He likes to know what things are and how they work. He can't help looking into boxes, on shelves, in corners, behind things, feeling objects, lifting, pushing and all manner of inquiring and exploring behavior to know better who he is and what the whole world is like. Knowing what words are and how that whole business works is just another natural question as far as he is concerned. The fact that the answer he seeks will really unfold over months and years is of no concern to him. He is simply and honestly interested. Can parents respond less honestly?

A parent's hesitation and putting off the child's inquiries *create the first self-doubts* for the child about his ability to understand and learn to read! Even his *first* questions lead his parents to tell him he'll have to wait until he's in school to learn to read. It must be terribly difficult, he thinks, and his first apprehension about learning to read is implanted.

There is no problem about the child's mind being strained or overtaxed in early reading. Of course, a parent could ignore all good advice and behave atrociously while acting as a teacher—require the child to keep trying far beyond the sensible fifteen to twenty minutes a day; persist in spite of tears and all. But, few would be so foolish or demanding.

What kind of proposition would reassure a concerned parent that his four-year-old has the basic mental capacity for handling this new skill of attaching sounds to letters of the alphabet; for learning the names for a basic sight vocabulary of whole words; and for arranging letters to make words or for fitting words together to make sentences? There are some obvious clues. The fact·that the child has already learned the names of many relatives, neighbors, shopkeepers, gas-station attendants, religious-school teachers and others should be convincing that he could learn the sounds or names of twenty-six different letters with some attention and practice. Each has its own characteristics, as people do. In the past year he has probably learned that many new names of candies, toys, games, sodas, snacks—or trade names on television—quite incidentally. He easily knows the names of 10 to 20 items of furniture; 20 to 50 names of foods; 15 to 30 names of apparel; et cetera. He understands the principle of individual and different examples for a class or type of items. For the class of letters, he needs to learn twenty-six individual and different examples. Naturally, sounds, names and capitals will become involved.

We already know that his vocabulary is rapidly expanding. He is going to continue to attach new sounds to new objects, regardless of what you do. When he is naturally interested is the time to start on the sounds of letters and some words.

Your child's level of general intelligence can provide reassurance as to his ability to attach sounds and meanings to objects and symbols all around him; you do not have to wait for pragmatic evidence. In the past fifteen years, significant new efforts have been made to understand the development of human traits and characteristics, including general intelligence. The rate at which general intelligence develops and changes has been the subject of scientific study for years. More recently, significant efforts have been made to examine the major studies of this century and to draw important conclusions from them.

By the time your four-year-old reaches age seventeen you expect him to be a well-developed adolescent, able to perform many skills and knowing a good deal about the world. In fact, that is near the age he may expect to be entering college. If we could take age seventeen as a theoretical 100 percent level of his development, we could express certain traits and characteristics at earlier ages as a proportion of that expected total. For example, we might be able to know at what age his height would be one half of that to be expected at age seventeen; at what age half of his expected maximum general intelligence would be developed. A very important study has done just that—generally drawing on and synthesizing significant related studies of human traits and characteristics over the past fifty years.[1]

What fraction of the expected general-intelligence level of your seventeen-year-old do you think might be needed just to learn the sounds and names of the alphabet letters? Or to begin to use them in decoding some words? How much would be needed to be able to recognize fifty basic whole words by sight? Would it be 10 percent, 20 percent, 25 percent? The fact of the matter is much more encouraging than that. Professor Bloom concludes: "In terms of intelligence measured at age seventeen, *at least 50 percent is developed by age four.*"[2] An additional 30 percent is added by age eight, and 12 percent more by age thirteen. Obviously, the parent need not be apprehensive on this score; the average four-year-old has a general-intelligence level far above what is required for learning the basics of reading.

Why bother a four-year-old with reading? Because he wants to know. He is ready to know. He is able to know. The sooner he begins to grasp the elements of reading, the more satisfaction and practice he will get. If you wait much longer, his enthusiasm for learning to read can wane. It is a continuation of the natural language experience between child and parent. He will be more interested in his environment. He will look for words and will reinforce his own reading development. He will occupy part of his day with constructive mental activity to balance his abundant play. He will form a positive attitude about reading instead of first anxieties about this complicated "reading thing" that his parents won't tell him about.

Some say there is nothing for a four-year-old to read if he does learn. They think only in terms of the daily newspaper, current magazines and the latest best-selling novel. The world is filled with suitable reading materials for the preschool child. Look in the supermarket and other stores. Look in your local library. Look around your house. Look at the books, games, puzzles and all kinds of early-reading matter. Many materials aimed at beginning reading and ranging on up are available. Any parent with scissors and paste can make homemade materials from newspapers and magazines. If the child has to, he will try to read anywhere he can find print.

Most people need to read to get information; to understand signs, announcements and warnings; to enjoy recreational reading; and to assist them in performing their jobs. Learning to read must *precede* these practical applications. The full learning process requires a few years. Ever so gradually, in an overlapping fashion, the uses of reading occur along with continued learning of the skill. The four-year-old is at the front end of learning the skill. Until he has developed some proficiency with it, he cannot make a general application of the skill. Yet, when he first shouts "Stop" on seeing a traffic sign with that word on it, he has begun the true application of the skill in his personal life. It should be obvious that most of the time, at first, must be devoted to learning the skill. Application and use will develop along with growing mastery. Application will find its own outlet as reading skill increases.

CAN PARENTS REALLY DO IT?

Not only can they do it, but they have been doing it for years. Not only *can* you, you *must* for your child's sake. Almost any parent who has a desire to succeed, who exercises patience and praise, and proceeds in a logical way, will teach his child to read before he enters school. Failure in this adventure will seldom be due to lack of mental ability of the parent. More often, lack of success will be related to emotional factors and misconceptions from failing to fully think through the task or to use common sense.

The median level of formal schooling in the adult population is just past the twelfth grade. More than one half of all adults have completed high-school attendance. Most of the other half reached the sophomore or junior year of high school, even if they dropped out at the end of the compulsory-attendance period, usually at age sixteen. Both general intelligence and formal schooling qualify the young parent basically for the teaching of beginning reading at home. The young parent's view is as important as the methods used. The basic view needed is one of surrounding the child with the kind of environment that will *draw out* reading skills. This is in sharp contrast to the concept of putting reading skills into him.

The parent does not need a course in reading instruction. He will, however, benefit from basic orientation to the task. He most needs to understand the type of climate that he must create for the child and the need for certain activities to be carried out. The parent's attitude and view of the mission are critically important.

You and your four-year-old at home, starting on the reading adventure, are in an entirely different situation from that of a six-year-old in a first-grade class at school with a teacher. *You have the better situation for developing reading!* You have a substantial advantage over the teacher in this challenge, if you are basically oriented (which is the objective of this book).

You have the natural first interest, readiness and enthusiasm of your child. You can work generally in a direct, uninterrupted, one-to-one relation with him. You can be much more flexible as to when in the day you wish to have a reading game or learning session (including the advantages of weekends and holidays). You can provide more kinds of praise, rewards and reinforcements. You know your child's every cue of attitude, emotion and behavior better than anyone else. You can forge ahead or hold back, as may seem best. You have only this basic skill to emphasize, instead of several other learning goals that compete for a first-grader's time and attention.

The typical mother of her first four-year-old is about twenty-two to twenty-four years old herself. If she has a second or third four-year-old, she is generally in the twenty-four-to-twenty-eight age range. Most directly, we are asking the question then, "Can a mother, age twenty-two to twenty-eight, be successful in teaching her preschool child to read?" The answer is yes. The mother is usually at least a high-school graduate. Many will have had some college attendance. Lack of success will seldom be due to lack of general intelligence for either the mother or the child.

Just how formidable is this challenge? A useful check list for you at this point will help determine your degree of interest and understanding of the general task that you will be undertaking (the last chapters provide specific recommendations):

1. Create and maintain a "reading-favorable" environment in the home.
2. Read to the child regularly, starting at as early an age as he shows interest in looking at books and listening to you read to him.
3. Be alert to the quality of his speech articulation and his visual acuity and in judging his readiness to begin reading by his questions.
4. Take him on short trips into the neighborhood, noticing printed signs and talking about them.
5. Control your own expectations; exercise patience; and dispense praise.

6. Provide plenty of writing and drawing materials and encourage more purposeful drawing and copying.
7. Be natural in your attitude and work with the child; be logical in your efforts.
8. Use only short time periods for learning and resist the temptation to extend them too soon.
9. Follow the principles of beginning-reading instruction (see later chapters) working with sounds of letters, the names of basic sight words and their individual sound elements.
10. Help the child create new words by rearranging letters and assembling words into simple sentences as rapidly as he shows an interest in these activities.
11. In case of doubt, use common sense.

WHY NOT LET A NURSERY SCHOOL DO IT?

Many parents believe that their preschool-age child shows real readiness for beginning reading, but they are sincerely concerned about providing only competent instruction to help him. Though they would be willing to take the time to work at it themselves, they would feel more secure if someone did the job in an institutionalized setting, such as a nursery school. Other parents, seeing the same readiness, would prefer to spend the money to hire the job done as a matter of convenience.

Two questions are faced immediately. Are nursery schools available? And if they are, will they provide the kind of instruction desired? The answer to the first question is that nursery schools in operation are far too few to serve the two- to five-year-olds who are their primary target population. Yet, most major metropolitan area telephone books list a few hundred "day nurseries" which include day-care nurseries, true nursery schools through the kindergarten level, and nursery-through-early-primary-grades schools.

A parent can find a nursery school for his child if he begins soon enough and persists in his search. But he will not find a school that will provide four-year-olds with a program of beginning reading.

The history of nursery schools accounts for their general nature. The nursery-school movement came to the United States from England, where it had developed out of a concern for the welfare of young children in slum areas of London. As early as 1918, the British government, by law, provided funds for services to children two to five years old. In 1920, nursery schools of the English type were established in the United States. Up to that time American nursery schools had been of the day-care type, largely accommodating the needs of working mothers.

By 1947, permissive legislation had been enacted in ten states for the operation of nursery schools using state, local and private funds. However, the basic objective of these schools was not and is not compatible with providing individual attention to beginning-reading skills.

The increase in number of nursery schools in the past fifty years has resulted more from the pressure to solve social and political problems than from a desire to serve educational needs. After the initial thrust in the 1920s, more nursery schools were added in the 1930s to help create jobs for unemployed teachers, nurses and others in the Depression. In the 1940s, the increase reflected the need to establish places where working mothers in defense plants could leave their children. In the 1950s, an educational motivation emerged, as a number of cooperative nursery schools were formed by parents striving to foster planned group experiences for children. In the 1960s, with federal funds under Project Head Start, many nursery schools were created to help alleviate the effects of cultural deprivation in the larger metropolitan areas.

At best, the nursery school (not day-care center) should be viewed as an ally of, and an adjunct to, the home and the role of the parent. Such institutions cannot provide many of the important and essential services the child needs in his developmental years. The general object of the nursery school has been to encourage social-mental development through a variety of experiences, exposures and materials.

Though particular emphasis in nursery schools may be placed on providing good oral-language models, beginning-reading experiences are not provided for four-year-olds. For less-than-five-year-olds there is a general readiness philosophy aimed at helping the child to be ready to conform to the more disciplined patterns of kindergarten and the first grade.

Nursery schools provide a socializing opportunity that many children would otherwise miss. Though children may become more generally alert, articulate and interested, they will not be introduced to beginning reading in any consistent fashion. A parent should not expect specific reading help for his child, in view of the number of children enrolled, their ages, their diverse needs and their different states of readiness. Nursery schools have their place and role, but they do not deal with beginning reading.

Several factors automatically argue against expecting reading help from a nursery school for your four-year-old: (1) the group situation and the teacher-pupil ratio effectively prevent the kind of individual attention needed; (2) the teacher is not expected to instruct in beginning reading; and (3) the few-days-a-week schedule for most children and the high absence rate of children for health and family reasons destroy the possibility of consistent daily reinforcements.

Brief reflection will bring you to the conclusion that the nursery school must be generally oriented to the whole group of children enrolled. The school is not organized to provide much individual attention, though equipment and materials are provided so that a child may be individually occupied. The amount of time possible for a one-to-one experience falls far short of that needed to generate a grasp of symbols and sounds required for beginning reading. Only a motivated parent can provide the condition for presentation of reading symbols, repetition, uninterrupted time, reward for progress, et cetera. The nursery school cannot.

As a young parent, then, interested and believing that your four-year-old should have the opportunity to begin learning to read, you have just one choice: do it yourself! If you wait until first grade, it will be too late to capitalize on the child's first interest and natural readiness; the "teachable moment" will have passed.

Now it all begins to come together! Without question, the average four-year-old is able, ready and willing to learn to read. Also, without question, there is no educational institution that will or can provide him with the individual attention required to proceed with the job. Further, if such instruction is not begun very soon, a pattern of subtle frustration can begin to form within the child over the refusals of help for something he has repeatedly inquired about. An apprehensive attitude about reading can develop. Certainly, the potential for disenchantment with his experience in first grade, when it finally arrives, is very great when he finds that the promise that he would learn to read "when you get to the first grade" isn't so easily kept.

Finally, the proposition becomes self-evident: the parent will teach beginning reading or it will have to wait its turn at age six. Common sense argues for the interested parent to begin. The naturalness of the home, the readiness of the child, the opportunity for regular reinforcement and reward, and the singleness of purpose argue for the parent to begin, rather than leave it for the teacher later, in the midst of less-desirable, group, at-school settings.

WON'T I MAKE A PROBLEM FOR THE SCHOOL OR MY CHILD LATER?

If you are tuned-in to the myths and prejudices about teaching your child to read early, you probably have a natural fear that by going ahead you will be creating a problem. You imagine that the first-grade teacher may resent your "doing the school's job" and that, in turn, she may take it out on your Johnny. You speculate

that your child will have to go through the beginning-reading
steps all over again, that he will be bored and your time and
effort will have been wasted. You wonder if it is good for him to
be that different from the other children. Finally, you are
bothered by the idea that early-reading children don't read any
better than the rest by the end of the third grade, anyway, so
why bother? How realistic are such fears?

In today's primary grades such fears are generally without
foundation. Of course, an occasional teacher could act unprofes-
sionally and irresponsibly, but the number of such teachers is
insignificant. It has been drummed into teachers of this genera-
tion repeatedly to expect differences in pupils and to plan instruction accordingly. Not only have teacher-education colleges
emphasized this philosophy, but in-service, on-the-job training
continues to push the theme. Professional literature emphasizes
the concept regularly.

Along with expecting individual differences, most schools do
something about it. Almost any school or school district's printed
statement of policy or philosophy will underscore this view.
Attention to individual differences is a cliché uttered by nearly
every school that appeals for support or strives to create a public
image. This view is universally reported early in conversation by
a teacher or principal in welcoming a new parent to the school. It
runs through most P.T.A. and parent meetings. Though the
theme may be overstated, there is genuine concern and action in
most schools to support the claim.

If there is a situation sometimes labeled as a problem, exactly
what is it? Essentially, it is the fact of a growing number of
pupils *entering* the first grade *already reading* at the level expected to be reached at the end of that school year. Because the
development of beginning-reading skill is the most important
declared goal of first grade, it is more surprising to find pupils
entering with the skill already developed than it is to find entering pupils with skills in such areas as mathematics and science.
Further, the historic myth about when one can learn to read
dramatizes the home's achievement all the more. The presence of

such children is a subtle psychological jolt to a profession that says reading should be taught at school. It is akin to having an appendectomy at home when everybody knows that you have to go to a hospital for it. Finally, it is a possible problem because it requires the first-grade teacher to work harder to provide realistic reading development plans at a second- and third-grade level in her classroom, too.

The basic question really is, how can the teacher provide for the top 10 percent *and* the bottom 10 percent of her class in terms of their quite different reading skills *and* for the large middle group so that growth and continued development for all will be assured? These differences can occur, too, in mathematics, science and other areas. They all require serious daily planning, instruction and evaluation. Most teachers try to deliver on this score. Some are hampered by compromising circumstances. A few are not equal to the challenge.

If the only realistic view over the next decade is that an increasing number of children will enter first grade at least one year advanced in reading skill, we should be aware of what many schools already do to work with the fact of such differences.

The most obvious effort, historically, to deal with the challenge has been to reduce the average size of the first-grade class and to increase the number of professional and other supporting personnel who make the first-grade teacher's service more effective. Even though the benefits of smaller class size are not scientifically proven, greatest change has been made in that area. First-grade classes are often given special consideration on class size when limited school resources force priority decisions. Over the past fifty years, too, there has been a substantial increase in the number of supporting personnel in schools—special-subject teachers, special-services staff, supervisors, curriculum specialists, nurses, clerical personnel, et cetera. Their service indirectly results in better learning by first-graders. If special teachers handle music, art and physical education, the first-graders' classroom teacher has more time for planning and evaluating progress in basic skills. To the extent that she can conveniently obtain advice and help on how to teach reading better, the teacher's skill will improve in that area. If a school librarian and a nurse are on the staff, the teacher gains still more time for helping her pupils. But additional personnel can never make up for lack of quality or competence itself in the first-grade teacher.

Grouping pupils for better instruction is customary. Teachers often create three or more reading groups on the basis of performance levels of the pupils. Sometimes a child, well-advanced, may go to another teacher or class for reading. Skipping a child ahead a grade on the basis of superior reading skill alone seldom occurs.

In recent years other plans of organization and staffing have been tried to adjust to the differences posed by children's rates of skill mastery. The use of teacher aides as nonprofessional helpers, usually paid, has freed the teacher's time for more direct professional contact with individual pupils. So-called "open classrooms," copied from England, are becoming more common; in these, children are permitted to pursue personal interests more at their own pace. Of most promise, but requiring more intensive curriculum organization and flexible teaching, is the "nongraded" or "continuous progress" organization of primary grades. Under this plan the lines between first and second grades, and sometimes between second and third grades, are dropped, thus creating an ungraded primary unit in which the child continues until he is ready to enter the next level of the school. Such an arrangement pools the talents of several teachers and staff members and focuses more attention on individual planning and evaluation. End-of-year promotion decisions are avoided. Academic progress is planned in a continuing fashion, depending on the latest level of achievement of the pupil regardless of the calendar or his classmates.

The variety of adjustments in first-grade instruction, organization, materials and staffing over the past twenty years is evidence of the active concern of teachers and school administrators with recognizing, and providing for, real differences in first-grade pupils and their continued progress. Differences, rather than being thought of as a problem, are accepted as a challenge to professional ingenuity.

Teachers expect some children entering first grade to read. If more do, it may actually help the instructional scene. It is a rare teacher who is so old-fashioned, unperceptive, lazy or rigid as to require early-reading children to repeat the beginning steps with the rest of the class. More likely, this child's teacher will be pleased with early progress and will provide the child with a more advanced set of readers and varied materials to challenge his interest and continue to develop his skill. From time to time a child may go through some entire unit with the class because he seems unsure of a particular concept. It will be a help to the teacher at the start of the year if the parent would let her know what has been accomplished at home. Occasional conversations through the year will permit the parent to continue the best plans at home to complement the school's new role in the child's reading.

Will you be making a problem for your child or the school if you provide early reading instruction at home? Certainly not, if you are at all logical about it. Does the school expect some children to enter first grade already reading rather well? Yes. Does the school expect individual differences in pupils and is it the school's business to provide for this fact? Absolutely; this is a fundamental assumption of most teachers. In fact, much of the change in early primary education over the past twenty years has been made because differences in abilities and skills (including reading) are expected in entering children.

The facts and common sense about the probable success of four-year-olds' learning to read at home and their later progress in school are so clear that any seriously interested parent should get started.

6

Deciding to
Start with
Your Preschool Child

By now your child is quite aware of the world of print. The newspaper at your door; letters and circulars in the mail; magazines at hand; advertisements on television; signs on buildings; your grocery list—all serve to impress on him now normal and usual print is. Even in less-advantaged homes, print shows on cans and cartons; bills come in the mail; advertising circulars are left; and television makes its mark.

Up to now you have helped your child generally to understand the value and function of words. He accepts printed words as a normal part of the environment and is increasingly curious about how you can figure out what they say. Aside from being read to, he has had only an informal and incidental exposure to print. From time to time, you have called attention to some especially interesting signs, words on television or ads in newspapers and magazines. From this informal exposure, before long, the child will want a more exact explanation about the different shapes of words and the letters in them. It is up to you, then, whether this normal interest will be encouraged or rejected.

Unless you are a prisoner of the myth warning that he must be six before he can learn to read, you have to make a decision as to whether you will begin to help him learn the meanings of word and letter symbols. First, though, you must make several observations about your child and some decisions about yourself. One or the other of you may not be ready to embark successfully on beginning reading.

ASSESSING READINESS TO START

Until your child is ready, there is little value in devoting time to helping him to learn to read. Being ready means that his interest is high enough, and his sensory and motor organs are mature enough, to justify your time and effort in terms of the learning that will result. Readiness means that his total condition is favorable for sustaining interest and making progress. To start too soon can be unproductive. Starting too late will miss the crest of his first interest and that advantageous teachable moment for beginning naturally. How can you determine when your child's readiness crest has arrived? Over a period of two or three weeks, by observation, you can watch enough of his natural behavior to draw a valid conclusion. In effect, you must diagnose his behavior. You must be alert to symptoms that reflect his degree of readiness. As in any responsible diagnosis, you must ask yourself some questions and look for answers in your child's behavior.

Four observations you make will be primary. Several others are secondary. Both types are important to your decision.

Vocabulary

Does your child have a large enough vocabulary to enable him to associate the form of a printed word with a meaning he already knows? The average four-year-old knows hundreds of words. For the next week or so, pay particular attention to the variety of words he uses. Engage him in longer conversations to satisfy yourself about the extent and variety of his vocabulary. You will probably be surprised about how many words he actually uses.

Hearing and Articulation

Speaking clearly and distinctly is necessary in learning to read. The child must learn the correct sounds for single letters and groups of letters. You will be helping him to learn the system of sounds for symbols. If he cannot hear you accurately and cannot reproduce almost the same sounds, he will not be able to connect the correct sound to a given word or letter.

Is his general speech clear enough now so that more refined attention can be devoted to individual sounds? Do people outside your family understand his speech? Get him into some new situations with friends or into shops where a person entirely unacquainted with your child can listen to him talk. Do they understand what he says? If not, he probably is not yet ready to work on sounds for letters and printed words.

Questions

The key indicator of interest in printed language is the child seeking help or explanations about words and letters. Has he asked yet to see his name? Has he asked the meaning of certain words? Has he asked about certain letters or has he pointed out some to you? These are key signals indicating genuine interest and curiosity. This interest will be necessary to maintain his effort in beginning reading. Maybe he has asked more than you realize. Listen for these questions over the next several weeks. Create situations that elicit such questions.

Visual Acuity

If a child can't see individual letters, he can't learn to read. The letters you are likely to use with him at first will be about one inch high. Can he now tell the difference between two similar things that are no wider than a half inch each? Can he tell the difference in detail between the two sides of a coin? Can he select from three similar buttons the one you describe by some individual feature of its shape or marking? Probably you have not had reason to think about his visual acuity seriously, yet. You must now. If you have any doubts after observing him carefully, he is not ready to start reading without an optometric examination.

The readiness indicators described above are critical. If you are doubtful about *any* of these conditions in your child, it will be unproductive for him to try to learn to read now, because a fundamental condition may stand in his way. You can more wisely devote time and attention to improving or correcting the condition you suspect. In the meantime, you should continue to provide general reading-favorable conditions in the home.

You may conclude that he must be encouraged to talk more, to enlarge his vocabulary; or that he needs to listen more attentively, to be able to reproduce word sounds more distinctly. He may need a better chance to exercise his share of talking within the family. You may conclude that an examination is needed to rule out or to correct a possible deficiency in vision or hearing. You may decide that you must bring more reading matter into the home and that family members should read to him more, to increase his interest in the process.

Aside from the four primary conditions just outlined, several secondary conditions must be observed, too. While each is important, none is critical in the same way that the previous group is. Should your child be deficient in any of these, give it attention and act to promote its development while you are starting with his reading.

The degree to which your child possesses, understands or exhibits the following traits has a bearing on how well he can profit from help that you will be providing:

—Is he attentive and can he concentrate on a specific task?
  Or, does he need encouragement and supervision to stay

with a job for a reasonable length of time (15–20 minutes)?

—Can he follow simple directions? Can he listen to, remember and carry out easy instructions?

—Does he spend some time independently most days looking at pictures and print in magazines, books, et cetera, around the house? Do you encourage such an interest by leaving reading material with pictures easily in reach and approve such browsing? Do you invite his attention to interesting pictures and talk about the words?

—Can he remember the general idea of a story and the major events in it? Do you talk with him about what you read together so that he has to think about the story? Can he talk with you about what happened in it?

—Does he understand basic concepts of direction that you will need to use in pointing out small but important differences in words and letters? Does he understand top and bottom; up and down; over and under; open and close; front and back; start and stop; first, middle and last? Does he have the idea of left and right and that you read his story books and words from the left side to the right side of the page? Does he understand the concept of sequence—arrangement of things in order, one after another, such as the pages of a book or letters in a word?

—With some practice, can he copy simple outlines of a house, a tree, a flower, et cetera, fairly well? Can he color a geometric figure within its outline reasonably well? Can he draw a fair circle the size of a penny and a reasonably straight line of an inch or two? Can he hold a picture book and turn the pages individually?

How well your child possesses each of these secondary traits is important to his progress in learning to read, in recognizing basic letter and word forms, and in associating them with their meanings. Each of these traits can be improved with practice and encouragement.

WHAT IS READING FOR A FOUR-YEAR-OLD?

Before we go any further in considering you and your child taking up beginning reading together, we should establish a definition of the reading goal that is possible. We are most concerned with developing the basic qualities necessary for understanding and beginning to manipulate printed language.

He must learn to associate some word meanings he already has with the printed symbols that represent them. He must learn to associate basic sounds with their individual letter symbols and a few combinations of letters. Eventually, he will learn the individual names as well as the sounds of the letters. He will need to grasp the concept of arranging and substituting letters to make different words and to produce different meanings. The time-line required to achieve these goals will vary with the individual child and with the nature of the guidance you provide.

Defining "reading" is still a controversial matter among reading specialists. Part of their quarrel is related to the fact that reading is a progressively unfolding, complex skill. Therefore, defining reading for a high-school or college student involves dimensions not essential for the beginner. Most simply put, *reading* means the ability to derive meaning from printed words. Obviously, there can be many levels of sophistication for such a process. In the beginning, we are concerned only with the rudiments of the skill. Progress will seem slow though "reading" actually takes place whether it involves a single word or an entire novel. Fully developed later, reading will include the subskills of perception, comprehension, interpretation and application.

Part of reading depends on memory and instantaneous recognition of words from overlearning. True independence in reading, however, requires the ability to analyze a word whose form and composition are not known in order to arrive at its name or sound as part of the reader's spoken vocabulary. Drawing *meaning* from printed symbols, not just sounding words, is the essence of reading. In the beginning, psychological support and self-confidence will be enhanced by mastering a growing list of words that are learned and are useful primarily as whole words.

First-Year Goals

For the first year of effort with a preschool child who is ready to read, the following goals are practical and attainable:

- —ability to speak clearly and to hear the different sounds appropriate to the individual parts of words;
- —recognition of several dozen words on sight without need to analyze the sounds within them;
- —knowing the symbol and sounds for most letters of the alphabet in lower-case form and most of their capital-letter forms;
- —knowing the vowels, *a, e, i, o,* and *u,* and their short sounds;
- —ability to copy acceptably all the letters he has learned and to print the correct one for a sound he says; ability to copy individual words and to form a simple sentence;
- —understanding of the idea of changing letters around and substituting one letter for another to make a new word;
- —ability to print his own name and a few other words from memory;
- —ability to read simple stories within the range of his sight vocabulary and increasing success in figuring out unknown words that are spelled logically;
- —possession of a "library" of books and homemade reading materials, keeping them where he wants, and using them independently with satisfaction.

Next Goals

After one and a half to two years of systematic effort with your child—that is, generally up to the time he enters first grade—he should

—have more than doubled his sight vocabulary from the first year;

—know all the letters of the alphabet (lower case and capitals) by sound and name, with some knowledge of certain alternate sounds such as *c* in "cat" and *c* in "city";

—have some ability to independently analyze printed words he doesn't recognize by using his knowledge of similar-appearing words, sounds of first letters of the word, how the word is used in the sentence (context), and sounds of final letters of the word;

—be able to copy legibly in manuscript style (see Appendix A) and compose sentences;

—be aware of how words can be made into other words by changing their first letters, last letters or their middle letters;

—know the long sounds for the vowels;

—know some of the common blends of beginning and ending consonant letters and their words (*bl, gr, th,* etc.).

Measured against present reading expectations for beginning first-graders, the achievement outlined above is easily comparable to a one-year advance in reading ability. Your child can achieve this result through moderate daily practice under your guidance and find it pleasant, exciting and satisfying. During the experience, he will have the exceptional advantage (as he did with speech) of being able to concentrate largely on the basic skill of reading without competition from other academic goals normally pursued at the same time as beginning reading in first grade. Equally important is the probability that, having acquired basic reading concepts at home, he will avoid the possibility of becoming a handicapped beginning reader at school later. There the teacher must keep the whole class moving ahead and may not have enough time to observe a particular problem or to give as much individual help as may be needed. In effect, your planned, systematic effort creates a kind of insurance that your child will not become a handicapped reader.

There remains, of course, the possibility that you will not carry through long enough or systematically enough in the preschool years to achieve the goals outlined above. What then? Fortunately, learning to read is an instance where a little knowledge is a good thing. So long as you have been logical and patient, the child can hardly be harmed, even though you may not help as much as you intended. If anything, you will have stimulated his interest and he will continue with questions until he gets more help from you or someone else—or figures out more things about print for himself. His interest in words and print will not disappear. This interest will seek to be nourished in some way. There is no way for the child to go backward!

The one- and two-year-goal descriptions are meant as general targets and average expectations. Normal differences among children will cause some to do better and some to accomplish less. Also, it would be a mistake to assume that his learning will go ahead in a linear fashion (i.e., an equal amount of progress in mastery for each week of effort). Just as in learning to talk, there will be a lot of early effort with little apparent result while the child is mentally digesting all he is hearing and seeing about words, letters and sounds. Plateaus in progress and new spurts will occur. The last three months of the first year will be dramatically better than the first three months in terms of demonstrated mastery and knowledge. Forget the goals and carry out the suggested activities positively and consistently.

ASSESSING YOUR READINESS TO START

So far, we have assumed that you are interested in helping your child and that you have the basic ability and temperament to do so. This may be a mistaken impression. Real success in introducing your child to reading also depends on you. Though you cannot start successfully until your child is ready, neither can you begin successfully unless you have a constructive view of the process and a positive attitude about what to expect. Though you don't need special skills, you do need a point of view and a plan, if you are to be successful. Let's look at you somewhat as we looked at your child earlier.

The degree to which you possess, understand and exhibit the following traits or have considered the following questions has a bearing on your ability to develop early reading skills in your child.

Inventory

Have you carefully observed your child and objectively considered the assessment items presented earlier? If there is some basic deficiency of speech, vocabulary, vision or hearing, put off starting now and correct that condition first.

Expectation

Remember how you naturally expected your child to learn to talk? You must have the same confident attitude about his reading. Recent investigation has borne out findings as to the significant role that a teacher's expectation plays in her pupil's actual learning.[1] Your expectation that the child will succeed will be conveyed subtly to him in ways that you will not realize. A kind of self-fulfilling prophecy works. If you doubt his success, or yours, he will sense it and his effort will be diluted.

If you start, you can have no doubt that your child will learn to read. He will never expect otherwise. But, make no mistake about it, you cannot "wish" him to success. Learning to read will require systematic, planned effort, though it won't be nearly as demanding of time as it was in teaching him to talk. He will mirror your optimism and your confidence, and will keep trying as long as you persist that way. If you expect success, you will probably see it come to reality. The reverse of this concept is often demonstrated in the inner city with minority and disadvantaged children in schools where a teacher may lower her level of expectation. It shows, and even the children who should make normal progress don't.

Praise

If your family tells you that they particularly like the way you prepare a certain dish or recipe, you are inclined to serve it again. If every time you played golf, as a beginner, your partners criticized your swing and laughed at your score, you wouldn't go back to the golf course very often. We all respond better, over the long pull, to praise and compliments than we do to punishment and criticism. So it is with children learning to read. There is no way to browbeat, force or shame a child into learning to read. Such behavior on your part will only result in his wanting to avoid the experience with you and to leave books and printed matter alone—not because he can't learn to read, but because you make the experience so emotional and unpleasant. Consistent encouragement, praise for *any* progress, and your expectant manner will inspire him to continue his effort and progress.

Praise can be overdone, but it cannot be done without. What may seem like a small achievement to you may be a very large step for your child. How soon would you become discouraged in learning a foreign language if the person helping you never complimented your effort or progress, or if you heard twice as much criticism as compliment? Bragging to other members of the family on any good point achieved helps support the child's effort and progress.

The old adages of "sugar draws more flies than vinegar" and "nothing succeeds like success" are apt for learning to read.

Patience

Good teaching always requires patience. The step from not understanding any language symbol to knowing just a few is a large one. Fortunately, progress accelerates as each new step builds on the ones already taken. Twenty minutes is not long for you to be patient at any one session. It is better to stop for the day, or not to start at all, if you aren't going to be calm, confident and interested.

Schedule

Short, regular sessions are the key to progress. A fifteen- or twenty-minute session daily is enough for the first few months. You will have to judge later whether another short session in the other half of the day is possible. The child's temperament, your style and his progress are the signs to watch. A single session twice as long will not get you twice the result; more likely, you will end up with less result than the short session produces. Try not to skip any day, even on weekend or holiday. By this plan you are following the psychological principle of distributed learning (daily and short), which is superior to massed learning (less frequent but longer sessions).

Learning isn't work for the child unless you make it that. After all, he wants to learn to read and you want him to. It is a fascinating mystery that you are unlocking for him. Why make it a matter of work? Don't press your luck to see if you can squeeze out just one more point from today's session. Quit with a compliment, before the child becomes too restless or you become impatient.

Environment

Even though you have regular learning sessions, you still need to support a total reading environment in and out of the home. Your child will have more chance to apply and reinforce new reading skills if you do. His pleased discovery of letters and words he knows will be a small reward for your efforts, too. Continue to "discover" signs in stores. Enlist other members of the family in the activity you have undertaken. They must become part of his total reading environment. They can bring home interesting examples of pictures with print. They can be interested in and praise small progress that you report or the child demonstrates. A little imagination will greatly improve the printed-language atmosphere around your new learner.

Teaching

Your basic attitude about what you are trying to do is quite important. Do not think of yourself as knowing something that you are somehow going to pour into your child's head. Think of the experience as a challenge to see how much of his talent you can develop, draw out and get expressed. You are trying to stimulate the dawning of a new understanding in him. You are not trying to have him please you or do something for you. You are trying to help him understand a mystery. He will have to make his own mental connections at his own pace, but they will be greatly influenced, hastened or slowed down by what you do.

You must be systematic and logical. You are not going to accomplish much by sterile drill, though regular and serious reviews of past learning will be productive. A machine that just showed him letters and words with accompanying sounds could produce a certain amount of learning. The fact that another human is working with him causes him to learn with meaning and to enjoy the experience, with better learning results.

If you get yourself reasonably ready with a simple plan and plain materials, and keep his attention, you can hardly miss being successful.

A good guide—which is really what you will be—first must be concerned about the well-being of his companion in a fascinating wilderness—which is what printed words are to a young child— regardless of how well the guide knows the territory and could hurry on by himself.

WEIGHING YOUR DECISION

Once your friends hear that you are working with your child on beginning reading you will get a variety of reactions—not just a repeat of the myth and prejudices described in earlier chapters, but more specific warnings and worries about how you are doing it and whether you really should. The last chapters provide a straightforward approach as a general guide for you. Always, in case of doubt, trust your own common sense. There is no magic formula that you will be violating. But, you should know something about the debate that continues to rage over beginning-reading methods among reading specialists and educators, and has given rise to so many views.

Not only has the general topic of reading been more researched and reported than any other in education for fifty years, it has been more persistently debated and argued over than any other facet of the curriculum. Many methods and procedures have been put forward. Fragmented research lies all around us. Entirely too little research has been conducted with children of preschool age and too little after the third-grade level. Over the past half century it would have been logical for professionals to plan and carry out longitudinal research to observe in the later school years the consequences of particular beginning approaches. Reading, being the most fundamental of all academic skills, and its mastery, being critical to the individual's success and satisfactions in life, should have received the commitment of significant money from foundations and the federal government. Today, there is the same basic need for organized longitudinal research and adequate national funding.

Because there have been so many exponents and publishers of particular approaches to beginning reading, one writer has reviewed the field and has identified at least one hundred approaches, arbitrarily classifying them into ten broad categories.[2] The fact of ten general *categories* itself is a compliment to the remarkable adaptability of young children in that they are able to learn something from each of them. Though each general approach has its disciples and fervent leaders, and though major publishing houses have invested tens of millions of dollars in developing basal reader series and other approaches, there is no agreement among the professionals on how beginning reading should be taught to obtain best results.

Fortunately, in the face of such mixed practice, about 75 percent of our children do learn to read reasonably well, finally, at school. No one knows how much anxiety and distress are experienced by many of the 75 percent while they are en route to becoming acceptable readers. To have about 25 percent, however, who do not learn, is a crippling statistic. It is a 100 percent tragedy for each child concerned. And, there is no way to know beforehand *which* child will wind up in the 25 percent having reading problems. Intelligence level is no guarantee of eventual reading success; but some knowledge of reading symbols *before entering the first grade* is the trait most often associated with reading success at the end of the first grade!

If there is something basically wrong, it must be corrected. With so much time and money spent over all these years trying to teach millions and millions of children to read, it has become critical that an effective approach or a few approaches be proved and used. However, in the light of normal differences among children, no one approach is likely to be always satisfactory or universally effective.

If there is any single feature basically wrong, it is our late start. This writer suggests, for reasons amply set forth in earlier chapters, that waiting until the child reaches age six before we teach him beginning reading in group situations wherein reading has to compete for the child's attention with all the other first-grade subjects is an irrational plan imposed on us by tradition and historic assumptions that must be completely re-examined. Further, that situation has been compounded by seriously neglecting the professional preparation of primary teachers for the teaching of beginning reading.

Is the help recommended in this book to parents just one more variation along with the one hundred approaches that were cited earlier? No, the guidance offered in the last chapter is based on the *principles* that are most often involved in the more successful facets of beginning reading and the nature of the four-year-old.

The most hotly debated issue in the field is whether a "phonics approach" or a "sight word approach" should be used. The wisest view seems to be that neither alone is best and that elements of each have their place in a logical, common-sense analysis of the time-line for developing beginning reading. In this connection, an important analysis was completed and reported a few years ago. It reviewed major research studies of the past fifty years that compared different approaches to beginning reading.[3] The report was based also on interviews with proponents of various reading approaches and observations in many classrooms. The author concluded that the main question at issue was whether beginning reading should be "meaning emphasis" oriented or "code emphasis" oriented. That is, do children learn better with a beginning method that stresses meaning or with one that stresses code. Code emphasis means mastering the basic alphabetic code first. Meaning emphasis means stressing whole words and groups of words for meaning without analyzing word structure by the letters or sounds involved. The study concluded that most children are currently learning by meaning emphasis but that a code emphasis could improve beginning reading at the start of school.

What appears later, as a guide for parents, is based on a consideration of what a four-year-old is like; the major elements involved in initially grasping the nature of printed language; the complications imposed by group teaching of reading in the first grade; the general motivation and competence of young parents; and the ease with which the necessary materials can be made at home or can be obtained.

The guidance offered later rests on the demonstrated success of a parent in developing functional speech in his child; the natural interest of the four-year-old in reading and his readiness to begin; the advantage of the direct, one-to-one learning situation at home; the personal interest and commitment of the parent; the ease with which elementary stimulus-response forms of learning can be employed; and the effectiveness of systematic, short learning experiences.

Unfortunately, most of the research assumes that beginning reading must be taught in a school setting, by teachers, to six-year-olds. One reason for our continuing problem has been our unwillingness to question that assumption. The idea of four-year-olds taught at home by parents is a perfectly sound premise, too. Our longtime difficulties with the first premise should encourage us, by now, to an objective consideration of, and organized experimentation with, the other premise.

If your child, though, is one of the eight to twelve million who will become four years old within the next two or three years, you can hardly wait for additional research proof that would make you more comfortable. You will have to make your decision on facts and common sense now.

7

What Is
the Best Plan?

The parent who wants to help his preschool child to learn early to read needs to know what to do and needs to do it systematically. The first logical question that comes to mind is, "How is it done at school?" If there is a generally accepted and successful way of teaching reading at school, the same method might be used earlier at home. Is there such a method?

READING IN THE FIRST GRADE

The usual way of teaching reading in schools today became popular after the end of the Second World War. In that period of a burgeoning birth rate, the very competitive publishing industry refined and expanded the concept of the "basal series" for teaching reading. Such a plan offered a school district a coordinated series of materials for teaching reading through a progressively expanding vocabulary starting with readiness activities at the kindergarten level up to the sixth grade and beyond.

Bursting on the scene as they did in the postwar struggle to capture the lucrative reading-textbook market, the colorful, "scientifically based," written-by-experts basal series were heavily merchandised. They were appealing to curriculum directors, teacher-selection committees, school administrators, and boards of education. The detailed manuals to guide teachers seemed a blessing for new and relatively inexperienced teachers, who were being recruited by the thousands to staff new classrooms.

The highly illustrated and colorful readiness materials, primers and beginning readers seemed naturals for increasing children's interest beyond that of the more prosaic books used formerly. The idea of a controlled vocabulary, progressively introduced and used as the mainstay for print in the readers appeared to "guarantee" the child's ability to read anything that had been learned as a whole word beforehand. The fact that a controlled whole-word vocabulary limited the scope of independent reading and out-of-classroom use was neglected in light of the refreshing new materials for young readers. Phonics and word-analysis skills for breaking the print code were generally delayed or appeared casually as part of the over-all integrated activities that were recommended *after* whole-word meaning was developed.

Two major publishers of basal series captured about 80 percent of the national market and have prevailed for the past twenty years. Most children in beginning reading over the past two decades have progressed through a readiness booklet starting either in kindergarten or first grade and then through pre-primers, primers and readers, at the pace prescribed in the teacher's manual. By the end of the first grade a child had been exposed to three hundred to four hundred words, but he had little knowledge of letter sound-symbol association. The process produced a happy, colorful, conversational experience as the controlled vocabulary was carefully fed out up through the third-grade level. A heavy emphasis was placed on the meaning of new words and learning to recognize them as isolated wholes before they were seen in stories. Little writing was developed through the first grade, and phonics orientation and practice were minimal.

Though the basal series were shaping the way most children were learning to read, other publishers put out a variety of plans. Some were imitations of the basals, others presented a substantial range of methods. The range was all the way from concentrating on the sounds and names of alphabet letters first to the basal's concentration on whole-word learning, to the neglect of phonics and writing. A nagging concern from some parents and others persisted, though, as to why there wasn't a greater emphasis on phonics and word analysis. Was it really good for the child, in the long run, to emphasize a sight vocabulary and to buoy up his interest artificially with multicolored illustrations and routine, unchallenging stories imposed by the controlled vocabulary? The pendulum has been moving more recently toward greater concern for phonics and word analysis, even in the new editions of the basal series.

There is, then, no nationally used, available and accepted method of teaching beginning reading for a parent to use with his preschool child. This, however, need not deter an interested parent, since identifying *the principles* that are productive is really what is important.

COMPARING METHODS

Has the whole field of reading been left in the hands of the publishers and their hired experts? Has there been no attempt to appraise the whole matter of what has been happening? With so many marketed methods for the teaching of beginning reading, there must have been some attempt to sort things out and to identify superior practices that produced better results. So many variables are involved in such an effort that little has been done. The most ambitious effort was carried out in the middle 1960s. Its findings are very important to parents interested in teaching early reading.

In 1964 the U.S. Office of Education funded a coordinated beginning-reading research program involving one thousand classrooms in twenty-seven different research projects.[1] The goal was to study major first-grade reading programs and to compare their effectiveness. The total effort was designed so that the entire plan could be analyzed as one mammoth study.

The study essentially researched two broad categories of approaches to the teaching of beginning reading: (1) the basal-reader series approach; and (2) nonbasal approaches. Five individual methods in the nonbasal category were assessed. Each of the five nonbasal approaches was compared with a basal program in each of the projects. Further description of the research design is not essential here, except to note that all the major variations in use in the 1960s for the teaching of beginning reading were being compared for relative effectiveness under impartial supervision.

The major conclusion of the entire study was that reading achievement of first-grade children is more closely related to the *situation* in which they are taught than it is to the general *method by which* they are taught! More differences in achievement among all the classroom groups were found *within* the results for any one reading method than were found to exist *between* the methods themselves. There was, then, more difference attributable to *how* a teacher used a single method than was attributable to the method itself as against any other method! For the person seeking that "one best method" this is a discouraging finding. Yet, at the same time, it emphasizes the importance of the role of the person guiding the young reader.

Where greater reading achievement was produced, regardless of method used, the teachers generally had better organized classes; they encouraged more active participation by their pupils; and they acted promptly to help a child correct a problem before it got too fixed. These traits of teachers getting best results were not necessarily related to how long they had been teaching or to their original professional training. Fortunately, an interested parent can model his own behavior on these traits at home.

Several of the findings and conclusions of the study, paraphrased for simple reporting, are important for parents' attention:

METHODS

1. No approach to beginning reading can be considered as best in all situations.
2. Children learn to read by a variety of materials and methods.

3. Combinations of approaches often are superior to a single approach.

PUPILS

1. Younger children achieved somewhat better than their older classmates.
2. Girls tended to be more ready at the start of first grade and tended to read better at the end of first grade.
3. Pupils who knew letter names before they entered first grade and who could discriminate between word sounds achieved better under every method of instruction.

GENERAL

1. Word-study skills must be emphasized and taught systematically.
2. Writing practice is helpful in learning sound-symbol relationships.
3. Teachers should be more expectant about pupil success.
4. The initial reading vocabulary should include both regularly spelled words and high-utility words.

What are the implications of this national study for parents wanting to help their preschool child at home as early as he is ready?

1. There is no one method to use that will be the *right* method.
2. Observing certain principles is more important than following any particular method.
3. Stimulating an early knowledge of letter forms and their sounds helps lead to later first-grade reading success.
4. The person teaching must be systematic in developing word-study skills.
5. Helping a child to learn to print letters and words while he is learning to read will help him to know the sound-symbol relationships.
6. The person guiding the learning must be positive and expectant about achieving results.

7. Both regularly spelled words and naturally used words should be a part of learning to read.

There is nothing mystical or guaranteeing in any of the methods used to teach beginning reading to first-graders. Therefore, identifying the important principles that are involved in various methods is the best guide for interested parents.

ADVANTAGES AT HOME

Parents with ready preschoolers have several enormous advantages for the teaching of beginning reading. These advantages, coupled with the principles of learning to read, will produce definite early progress in reading:

1. You know your child better than anyone else does. You understand his behavior, moods, likes, dislikes and needs. No teacher will understand him as well as you do.
2. You can judge best his readiness to begin reading from what has been stated in earlier chapters or just when he arrives at that readiness point.
3. You can work with your child consistently in a direct, intimate, one-to-one learning situation. He need not wait for personal time from a classroom teacher or continue to repeat an unnoticed error. You can adjust the over-all time or the nature of a specific activity according to the child's behavior and interest, which you know best.
4. You can foster his specific involvement and direct his learning. Your child need not be one of a group, waiting his turn or just being an observer. He can be directly involved all the time.
5. You can provide direct and immediate praise and rewards to reinforce learning behavior. You know the type of reward and praise that will be especially supportive. You have a greater range of tangible reward items and opportunities at hand.

6. You can provide more systematic instruction in a year in reading than the school can. While the school year (180 days, generally) is less than one half the days in a calendar year, you can teach reading at least 125 days *more*, even if you skip a day every week and most single holidays. The key to learning to speak was the continuous exposure to speech practice on a 365-days-a-year basis.

7. You can be systematic and use a regular time of day or you can adjust the learning period to another part of the day easily, for good cause.

8. Learning to read is likely to be the only systematic learning your preschool child is trying to acquire. He doesn't yet have to be concerned with learning arithmetic, music, art, who our "community helpers" are or other subjects in an ongoing systematic way. Of course, you will be exposing him to other learning, but reading is his one, systematic, daily, planned program.

It seems clear that no single method of teaching beginning reading need be used exclusively and, in today's schools, general qualities of a teacher as well as particular traits from professional training aid beginning readers. We already know that the average four-year-old is ready to read and that he can learn to read. We have just noted an impressive list of advantages the parent has at home for teaching his child. If we could identify the main principles that should be observed in learning to read, you could start with confidence.

GENERAL PRINCIPLES FOR PARENTS

Many children will not learn to read early, because their parents are afraid they can't teach them properly. These parents are too cautious. They let their own mental image of "teaching" intimidate them.

Parents should be reassured by the view of psychologist Dr. Jerome Bruner, of Harvard University. Over ten years ago he stated a position often quoted in educational circles: "Any subject can be taught effectively in some intellectually honest form to any child at any stage of development."[2]

A few principles are important in teaching a child to read. Most commercial reading methods rest on one or more of these principles. The fact that some children learn to read by *any* of the commercial methods shows that some of these principles are involved. The wide differences in achievement produced by commercial methods are attributable to the neglect of some principles and to variations in the nature of children and teaching.

The following principles *must* be observed if a child is to learn to read well:

1. A child learns best by mentally connecting what he does know with what he does not yet know.
2. A child learns best when several senses are involved in the process.
3. A child learns best when he understands the purpose of the learning experience and concentrates on it.
4. A child learns best when he is directly involved in the process.
5. A child learns best when the process is logical in terms of his readiness and the material to be presented.
6. A child learns best when his progress is reinforced by praise and reward.
7. A child learns best when he practices in a real situation and when review causes him to demonstrate previous learning.

Generally, these principles constitute a body of common sense that an interested adult would follow if he wanted to help a young child learn anything. A brief comment will help explain each.

Connecting the Known to the Unknown

Each of us learns by progressive steps, each of which must start with what we then know. When you tell a person how to get to a location that is strange to him, you always start with a landmark he knows or where you are. You give directions (i.e., *teach*) by associating the known location with the unknown location so that he can understand the relationship between the two in order to make the mental connection that will help him to understand. You may have to tell him more than once to establish the mental connection. So it is with a child learning to read.

The *only* point from which a child can start, at first, is his *oral vocabulary.* By connecting simple words that he knows with their printed form, a chain of associations will be started. Eventually, this chain and new understanding will provide him with knowledge of the sounds of alphabetic letters, their names, words recognized instantly on sight, and basic ways to analyze unknown words.

Involving Several Senses

Sooner or later learning to read involves hearing, speaking, seeing and writing. Generally, learning results from multisensory experiences more than we realize. Using more than one of our senses helps us to learn better.

When a child first learns the concept of "ball," he gets one impression by seeing it; another from holding it; another from rolling and bouncing it; and another from making a clay ball. Saying the word "ball" is just one of several sensory avenues to understanding. The total experience of all the senses helps him to understand and know "ball" best.

Actually, few things are learned through only one of our senses. The more senses involved, the better, usually, a concept is understood. So it is with print. Seeing the letter *b* is one experience; it is another when traced with a finger; another when it is handled as a three-dimensional form; another when it is written; and another when it is sounded. The idea of b is learned best from total experience with it through sight, sound, touch and writing.

Understanding Purpose

Most human behavior results from conscious purpose or from an unconscious need that must be satisfied. We work better at a task when we understand and agree with the purpose it serves. When an activity is meaningless or when we don't understand its purpose, our effort is less satisfying and less productive. Threats or force may obtain the desired behavior temporarily, but in the long run attention is diverted to the threat or imminent punishment instead of to the learning.

A preschool child wants to learn to read. He has a purpose, but he needs to understand that he must learn about letters, words and their sounds before he will be able to read a lot. Both the immediate goal of the day and the eventual goal of reading must be understood. It is important to remind him, at the end of each day's session, of progress being made in order to sustain his interest for the next session.

Being Directly Involved

The total nature of a situation dictates how much learning will occur. Active involvement of the learner in the situation is necessary, to heighten his concentration, his interest and his identification with the process. Both the duration and the quality of the experience are related to the child's sense of involvement. Merely repeating what is said or "going through the motions" listlessly will not produce learning at all and can even produce a negative effect.

A parent's comments are important to increase the child's involvement. The child may not be aware of his progress. He needs to know, for self-reinforcement and to remain involved. A child who is actively *involved with* the process has a great advantage over one who is only being *told about* beginning reading.

Being Logical and Systematic

Beginning each lesson at the point of a child's present knowledge is logical. Learning a complicated total skill comes about through mastery of a series of small separate steps which build on the knowledge gained in prior steps.

What is logical depends on the child's current knowledge at any given time. Logic also must govern the organization of the material to be learned. The various subskills in reading have a logical relation to one another. When their sequence and relation are ignored, the rate and quality of learning decreases. When the relation is observed, progress is more consistent.

Learning is supported when the learner is involved on a regular schedule. Short, regular sessions are the most productive. A session a day, at home, will produce observable progress.

Reinforcing Learning

One of the oldest laws of learning is that a response that is followed by or is accompanied by a pleasant state of affairs is likely to be made again. That is, if what the child does is rewarded in some way that makes him feel good about himself or benefits him, he will be likely to do it again. If the child's effort and progress in each of the learning steps is praised, he will tend to persist and will find satisfaction in the activity. If not, his interest and effort will diminish.

Occasionally, and for a short time, a desired response may be produced to avoid pain or punishment. However, punishment will help only briefly; in the long run, punishment will discourage learning.

Meaningful Practice and Review

Sheer repetition or rote practice will not necessarily increase mastery of a skill or understanding of a concept, but *purposeful practice* will. Practice must have the attention of the child and his feeling that it fits the purpose.

A skill is learned so that it can be applied either for its utility or for its satisfaction. The sooner such results are evident, the sooner practicing the skill will become self-reinforcing. As soon as a child can recognize a whole word by sight, he will gladly search for it (i.e., practice recognizing it) among strange words, just for the satisfaction of finding it. The sooner he can print the letter *b* correctly *in a real word,* the more his mental grasp of *b* will become permanent. Printing *b* as the first letter in five short real words that he can recognize can be more beneficial than copying the single letter many more times in isolation.

Review of recent-past learning is essential to the permanent fixing of concepts. Reviews should be regular but also natural and purposeful. Review confirms the degree to which past skills have been mastered and helps determine the rate at which new progress can be made.

A parent who follows the above principles will be successful in teaching his preschool child to read at home. In doing so, he will be seizing the best time in the child's life to introduce the reading code. The great advantage to be gained is the high probability that early teaching will permit the child to avoid becoming a handicapped reader later on, when he tries to learn to read with a group of children in a first-grade class. As an extra dividend, he will also be a better reader.

8

Early Reading –
A Plan and
a Foundation

You can teach your four-year-old to read. You will be surprised at how much reading progress you can stimulate by using the plan outlined in this book. By starting early and proceeding as outlined, you will avoid problems that frustrate many children later in the first grade. Even if your child is beyond age four and is in school now, but has not learned the essentials of reading, you can produce important progress by following the plan explained here.

This chapter provides the guidance that you need to be successful. There is no intent here to offer a detailed teaching manual. You don't need one! Common sense and initiative within the steps outlined are enough. Remember, you are helping your own child in a particular situation. With this book as a guide, following the principles previously discussed and using simple materials, you are in an excellent position to teach your child beginning reading. Each activity is sufficiently described to give you secure guidance.

CHECKLIST FOR STARTING

Before you start, review each of the following points repeated here from Chapter 6. In regard to critical primary characteristics, does your child:

1. have a good general vocabulary?
2. hear all right and speak clearly?
3. ask questions about words and print?
4. see small items and distinguish small differences?

In regard to important secondary characteristics, does your child:

1. concentrate and is he attentive?
2. follow simple directions?
3. enjoy looking at magazines and books?
4. handle books and turn pages by himself?
5. remember the general idea of a story?
6. understand directional concepts?
7. copy and color with reasonable hand control?

Your child must exhibit each of the primary characteristics before you start reading instruction. If he is weak in any of the secondary traits, arrange situations to strengthen them while you begin his reading program. Use any natural experiences that will give him practice in those characteristics and go ahead.

GETTING STARTED AT HOME

The list of skills you can expect to develop within one year may seem impressive at first. However, listing the goals individually makes them seem more formidable than they are. The list is your general guide and end-of-year goal. What other skill for your child could be more important to acquire over the next year? Don't worry about progress, just work consistently with the listed activities. Your child will begin to read if you are consistent and patient. Over the next year you can expect your child to

1. recognize several dozen words on sight;
2. be able to hear individual sounds within words he says;
3. recognize most of the letters of the alphabet in lower case and capital form;
4. copy letters accurately and sound them;

5. substitute and rearrange letters to form new words;
6. print his own name and several other words from memory;
7. read simple stories with satisfaction;
8. have some success in sounding out and decoding unknown words.

ORDER OF KEY SKILLS

Any complex skill must be learned by mastering its parts and gradually coordinating them. Attention must be focused individually on each subskill. Gradually, these parts will become integrated into the whole skill. So it is with learning to read.

Independence in reading can be developed only through mastery of the essential subskills. The beginning reader must

1. learn a modest number of words by sight;
2. learn to hear individual sounds as part of a whole word;
3. learn to associate the alphabetic letters that represent selected sounds;
4. practice printing individual letters and saying their sounds to reinforce letter-sound connections;
5. practice copy printing of words and short sentences;
6. understand that letters of a word can be rearranged or substituted to form new words;
7. apply sight-word knowledge and letter-sound skills to decode unknown words.

There is a logical order for taking up each subskill. The order is based on the principle that learning proceeds from the "known" to the "unknown" in developing skill mastery. The required skills have a definite relation to one another as each, in turn, becomes the known base from which the learner can move on to the next unknown subskill. The human mind is so capable that less logical orders can be followed but, *the most direct and least confusing sequence is shown above.* Figure 1 presents

Figure 1

RELATION OF SKILL GOALS IN
FIRST-YEAR ACTIVITIES

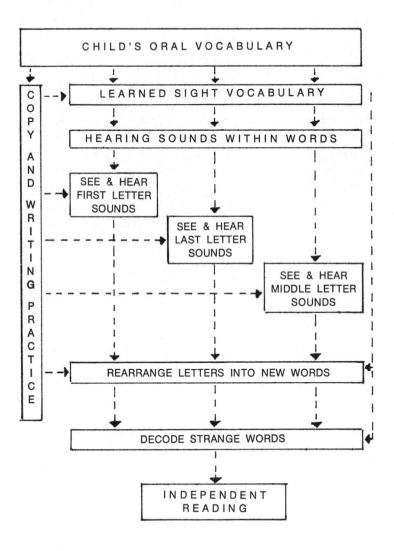

schematically this sequence leading from the child's oral vocabulary to his eventual ability to decode unknown words and to read independently.

The place to start is with words the child already knows and uses! The first step is to associate some of these words with their printed form *as whole words*. Learn the whole-word sound, just now. With rare exceptions (such as names of family members or special-interest words) these will be one- or two-syllable words. When several such words are known on sight they will become the raw material used in calling attention to the individual sounds that together comprise a whole word.

With practice in listening, the child's attention can be directed to the fact that he is voicing several different sounds when he says a single word. There are first sounds, ending sounds and middle sounds. When the child can become aware of individual sound parts of words, those sounds can be associated with the letters of the alphabet that represent them in print. Soon after the letter representing a single sound is the subject of attention, it should also become a small exercise in printing, so that the child will associate (1) the sound he makes, (2) the letter representing that sound in print, and (3) how to print the letter. Repeating the process (see later instructions) gradually develops the child's mastery of a growing list of sight words, all the letters of the alphabet and how they are printed. With a grasp of just a few letter sounds, including a few of the vowel sounds, he will be able to begin rearranging letters and understanding that these changes can make new words. *Now* the mystery of language is becoming more clear to the child, and he will experience his first sense of power at manipulating printed language!

The condensed description above outlines the logical progression from each skill to the next unknown subskill—all starting from a natural beginning with the child's own oral vocabulary. This is the most direct route for learning to read. Though the mind is capable of learning the artificial code order of the *a-b-c*'s first, that is an artificial approach without meaning to the child. It is a sterile drill of no present value to the child. Naming and reciting the order of letters in the alphabet has no relation to learning to read. This and other indirect approaches only introduce unnecessary and confusing steps for the child.

Figure 1 presents the most direct sequence of skills needed by beginning readers. A child's oral vocabulary and a learned sight vocabulary of words form the foundation for learning sound-letter associations—that is, *phonic skills.* Figure 1 shows that a sight vocabulary *and* phonic skills are necessary for reading! For the rest of the reader's life he will use sight words and phonic skills according to his needs. Where words can be recognized instantly by sight, they will be. Where words must be decoded, they can be. None of us reads solely by either method, nor should we need to do so.

There can be no fixed rate of progress. Children are different. Parents are different. Time devoted to teaching will vary. Each new subskill should begin as soon as success with it seems possible.

Figure 2 makes clear the order and general relation in time for beginning each new subskill. Several weeks should be devoted to learning whole sight words, copying word models and listening to sounds within words. As soon as twenty-five or thirty sight words are known, the sounds the child hears at their beginning and end can be associated with letters representing each. These letters, in turn, must be practiced through printing. The rate of mentally connecting letters with the sounds they represent will speed up between the second and the fourth month of effort. About the middle of the first year of systematic home practice, your child will probably be able to arrange letters with some skill, to form new words. In the latter half of the year those skills will be put to use in independent reading, in writing at his own level and in decoding unknown words—that is, *reading*.

To show and analyze subskills by chart and comment does not mean that they should be taken up in artificial time segments and dropped for the next stage. Each, once begun, must be practiced

Figure 2

GENERAL TIME FOR STARTING READING SUBSKILLS

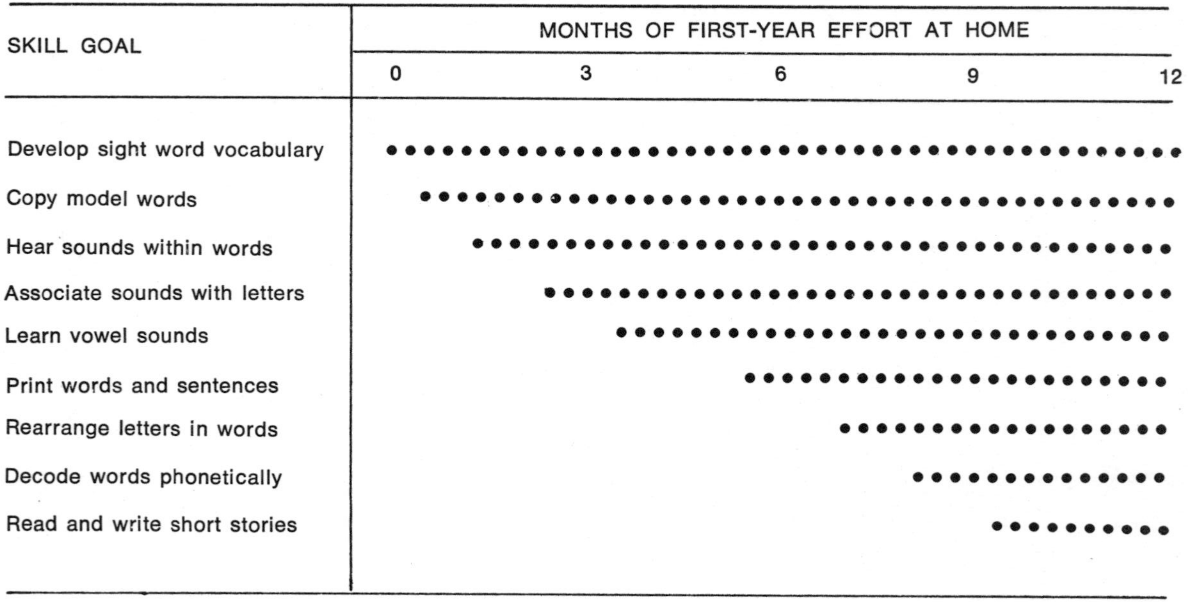

SKILL GOAL	MONTHS OF FIRST-YEAR EFFORT AT HOME				
	0	3	6	9	12
Develop sight word vocabulary	••
Copy model words	••
Hear sounds within words	••••••••••••••••••••••••••••••••••
Associate sounds with letters	••••••••••••••••••••••••••••
Learn vowel sounds	••••••••••••••••••••••
Print words and sentences	•••••••••••••••••
Rearrange letters in words	••••••••••••
Decode words phonetically	•••••••
Read and write short stories	••••

and reinforced throughout the year. For example, a child's sight vocabulary should be enlarged constantly. Listening to specific sounds and printing letters will continue throughout the year.

IMPORTANCE OF A SIGHT VOCABULARY

It is a very natural first step to help a child recognize in print some of the words he already pronounces. It is also logical to go from his spoken vocabulary by matching spoken words with their printed counterparts. The child will quickly understand that every spoken word has a printed form and that words are thought units of language—like single bricks which together make a wall.

After only a few weeks of regular work, a child will have a false sense of being able to read, just because he can recognize a few words on sight. Let him enjoy the feeling, because he really is reading, in one sense of the word. However, he could never memorize enough words by sight alone to become a proficient reader, so you must move on to understanding sounds and letters and their use in words. By knowing sight words, a child is laying the foundation that will help him to learn all the letters later in their natural setting—that is, within words.

Sight words must be those the child already speaks. Also, though he can say a good many multisyllable words, you should concentrate at first on words of one and two syllables. Their use later to illustrate individual sounds helps to determine which to select. Table 2 on page 140 presents a practical list of early sight words that will be particularly useful in teaching sound-letter associations.

A child's sight vocabulary is a pool from which examples can be drawn for illustrating particular sounds and letters in real situations. Three sight words are enough to deal with in a single twenty-minute session. In time, when those three seem almost mastered, introduce two or three more words to extend the child's skill according to the rate of learning he is showing.

Remember, forgetting from time to time is natural, so you must go back over words periodically (cheerfully) in review sessions. If the child has persistent trouble with a particular word, lay it aside. No single word is critical or worth tears. It can be brought up again later on—probably with success. Don't insist on mastery of every word as you go. If a child can recognize eight or nine of the first dozen words presented over the first few weeks, he is making good progress. His rate of progress will accelerate in time.

Table 2

USEFUL SIGHT-VOCABULARY WORDS

The following words make up two thirds to three fourths of all the words a child is likely to encounter in the usual reading materials of the primary grades. The words are largely operational or connote qualities of the language rather than being names, or nouns. Choose words beginning with different letters to give diversity to sight-vocabulary practice.*

(a)	by	come	down	fast
are	boy	cut	done	first
all	been	came	dog	four
as	bad	call	door	five
an	best	cry	drink	funny
any	both	cold	draw	full
ate	before	catch	deep	farm
am	because	clean	dinner	father
ask	began	could	**(e)**	found
again	back	carry	eat	flag
after	better	children	even	fish
about	between	change	every	**(g)**
away	bring	climb	eye	go
around	brown	club	early	get
another	blue	**(d)**	eight	good
across	black	do	**(f)**	give
(b)	beautiful	did	for	got
be	breakfast	does	from	gave
but	**(c)**	don't	fall	going
big	can	day	find	goes

* See also Table 4, page 152.

green	long	one	small	us
grow	live	once	start	under
glad	last	**(p)**	shall	use
(h)	lap	put	show	upon
he	light	play	stop	**(v)**
his	lunch	place	school	very
had	**(m)**	please	smile	**(w)**
have	me	people	store	we
him	my	pick	slow	was
her	man	pull	secret	will
has	made	pretty	**(t)**	what
how	much	print	to	who
here	may	**(q)**	the	with
hand	myself	quick	then	want
help	many	quiet	they	why
hold	must	**(r)**	them	when
home	more	ran	this	went
hurt	make	red	that	walk
hard	mother	ride	two	wet
house	morning	room	three	well
happy	miss	run	those	work
high	**(n)**	read	try	were
heard	not	right	take	where
(i)	no	round	too	which
I	new	real	there	would
if	name	**(s)**	thank	write
is	never	see	took	watch
it	now	so	time	water
in	next	sit	ten	warm
into	night	say	their	wait
its	nine	soon	think	wish
(j)	**(o)**	saw	talk	wash
jump	on	said	than	white
joy	of	she	tried	**(x)**
(k)	off	some	told	x-ray
kind	old	set	thing	**(y)**
keep	out	sure	tell	you
know	open	six	turn	yes
(l)	only	seven	today	your
let	our	side	tomorrow	yellow
look	own	soft	together	yesterday
like	over	sad	**(u)**	**(z)**
little	other	sleep	up	zebra
laugh				

* See also Table 4, page 152.

Sight words are learned by the simple process of sound-sight association and repetition. Present the few words you plan to emphasize in today's session through a made-up story. Then, print a two- or three-line story on a blackboard or big tablet to show them in print. Emphasize the target words when you read the story. Remember how television and radio advertising mentally fix particular trade names in mind by repetition?

Print each selected word on a 3x5-inch white card. Show it to the child. Say the word and have him repeat it. Turn the card over and do the same with another word, and so forth. Thereafter, repeat the words in the same manner. Finally, show the three cards in a one-two-three order *allowing time for the child to think* about the correct name of each. Before the child becomes too anxious or frustrated, say the word for him and have him repeat it again. Don't criticize. Time and repetition, not pressure and criticism, will bring results. Don't try for any particular pattern of sounds among the first words he learns. Use a variety.

Gradually accumulate a deck of 3x5-inch sight cards, making them with a black felt-tip pen or Magic Marker. Make the letters in lower case about one inch high.* Make two cards as you go along, so you can play a matching game with the child later to give him another kind of practice in noting word and letter characteristics. As time goes on, increase the number and complexity of his sight words.

There are about twenty short words that make up at least 25 percent of the running copy usually prepared for young readers. Work these into his sight vocabulary to enhance his reading power, because he will find them in many places. They are:

a	it	he	his	will
and	is	the	you	not
at	to	go	for	we
I	on	of	in	was

* See Appendix A for printing style.

Remember, some words in English are spelled so irregularly that they are better learned by sight as whole words. They aren't worth the effort to analyze phonetically (e.g., "eight," "through," "laugh").

Before going further, look over the following summary learning activities (Table 3) discussed so far in this chapter as a review.

INTRODUCING PRINTING

As soon as your child has learned eight or ten words through sight-vocabulary sessions, he should be encouraged to begin printing. He may already know his name when he sees it in print. Or, he may even know how to print (draw?) his name, by now. If not, remember that to him his name is probably the most fascinating single word in the entire language.

Ask the child if he would like to learn how to print his name— or the name of some other member of the family, a friend or a pet. The purpose is to introduce him to intentional use of a pencil and to begin practicing control of finger, hand and wrist muscles. Soon, he will need better control as he practices forming individual letters when he begins to associate sounds with their letters. Just now, though, he is not concerned with letters. You only want him to get some practice holding a pencil and *drawing a word.* You don't even need to use his sight words for this practice.

Use a few short words that are personally interesting to the child. Print a word at the top of a plain sheet of paper. Let him try to copy it. *Don't* say or spell the letters of the word! Just name the word itself and see if the child can make the marks or draw it as a whole word. You can use the blackboard for this practice, too. But, be sure the child also practices with a soft lead pencil on plain paper. Decide on a place that will be physically comfortable for this writing practice.

Table 3

DEVELOPING A SIGHT VOCABULARY

Activities

—Select three words to be learned.
—Tell a short story using those words.
—Print two or three sentences using the selected words.
—Point along the sentences as you read and underline the selected words as you clearly say each.
—Ask the child to say each word (point).
—Print each selected word on a 3x5-inch card.
—Show each card to child and pronounce word clearly.
—Have child repeat after you.
—Give child card and repeat practice.
—Try two cards, then three, a little faster; change order.
—Continue practice with interest and praise.
—Repeat process over several days until learned.
—Introduce new words as possible.
—Save all cards for review and evidence of progress.
—Make a matching deck for later games.

Materials

—3x5-inch white unlined cards.
—black felt-tip pen or black Magic Marker.
—blackboard at least 2x3 feet mounted or well propped up or large pad of paper or newsprint blank pads.
—see Appendix A for letter style.

Situation

—Use a daily 15–20-minute session.
—Select a quiet place to aid concentration.
—Work pleasantly; don't demand; settle for progress, not perfection today.
—Sit alongside the child, not opposite; have a helper attitude.
—Think about what you want to do before you start the session.
—Have all materials at hand for that session.

Compliment the child on whatever effort he makes. Encourage him to try longer. Praise any improvement you see. Let him practice as long as he wants (you may be surprised).

Again, don't start naming letters. The word is the whole name of someone or something. Let it go at that, just now. Attention to letters is not the object of this particular effort. The child literally is drawing a whole word. If he asks to practice more, let him. Or you may suggest practice. What new word would he like to try? He doesn't need to become a proficient printer on just one word.

Let the child practice printing as much as he wants to in addition to your sessions with him on sight vocabulary. Also, don't worry much about neatness, saving paper or making lines for him to print on at this stage. Don't be overly concerned about how the child holds the pencil or just how he decides to try to imitate your printed model. A little later, when you are working on particular letters, as such, you will follow the advice given in Appendix A about holding a writing instrument.

Don't confuse the child with too much advice at this stage. Let him enjoy "printing." Show the results, with praise, to some other member of the family or a friend, and get their praise of it too—in the child's presence.

9

Sounds
and Letters—
Writing
and Reading

Once a child has acquired a sight vocabulary of twenty to thirty words, he is ready to learn about letters and the sound that each represents in print. In only a few months he can learn a great deal about language in print and be reading simple stories with satisfaction. As a dividend, he also will be printing acceptably.

Learning to recognize several words by sight is the first mental bridge between known *word sounds* and previously unknown *words in print*. This new knowledge will be used soon to help connect mentally *individual sounds* with the symbols that represent them—*printed letters*.

You should not be tempted to teach your child the *a-b-c*'s, though doing so is possible. Even though a child eventually can learn to recite the names of twenty-six letters of the alphabet in order, what will he do with that skill to help beginning reading? It is *sounds*, not the names of letters, that you must work with first. The order of letters in the alphabet is unimportant at this early stage of printed-language experience. Letter names will work their way in quite naturally in time, as a matter of simple utility. You need not emphasize them.

FIRST LEARNED SOUNDS

Up to now, the child may not be aware that words he speaks are really made up of different sounds voiced in quick succession. He must have his attention directed to this fact. He must practice hearing a single sound as part of a word, so he can connect it with the letter that represents that sound in print. Becoming aware of the *beginning* sound of a word is easiest for a child. An *ending* sound is next-easiest to hear. Take up middle sounds last. Your purpose should be to help your child (1) to become conscious of the particular sound he says at the beginning of several words he already knows by sight; and (2) to be able to say just that beginning sound alone.

Say a few of his sight words (without showing them) and have the child repeat each one distinctly after you. Say the word at a natural speaking pace. Have the child mimic you each time. Repeat the word a little more slowly until the child is actually emphasizing the *beginning* sound for each word. Have him look into a mirror, if you wish, as he voices three or four words that begin with different letters. Help him to see that he is using his lips and mouth quite differently at the beginning of each word. For example, you might try the words, *hit, map,* and *rob.*

When you think he understands that many words start with different sounds, get him to say, after you, only the beginning sound of the beginning *h, m* and *r.* When you are satisfied, over several sessions, that he is aware that there are individual beginning sounds, try the same procedure for ending sounds. When the child can hear and say single sounds individually, you are ready to form the mental bond between any of these sounds and the letter that represents that sound in print.

Most words begin with a consonant. Don't use any words that begin with a vowel for this sounding practice. However, since no word in our language can be a word without including at least one vowel, you will soon have to pay attention to the vowels.

They will normally represent middle sounds in -words. Also, vowels should be learned at first only as their *short sound* such as *a* in "hat." Short-sound vowels appear much more often in our language than do long-sound vowels. Therefore, short-sound vowels are more useful to the child in early reading and decoding skills.

You should teach three or four consonant sound-letter combinations, as described below, before you attempt teaching two or three of the short vowel sounds. When you practice beginning, ending and middle sounds in words and their associated letters, you are starting to develop phonic skills so that the child will be able to "sound out" (decode) words he does not know on sight.

FIRST LEARNED LETTERS

Which letters to learn first—that is, to connect with the sound they represent—depends on which ones will be least confused with others in print and which ones will be of the greatest use because of the frequency of their appearance in primary-level reading material. For example, the letter *m* and the letter *l* are quite different in appearance. The letters *d* and *b* though, might easily be confused by a beginner.

Your purpose now should be to help your child (1) to associate a particular sound he can say with the letter that represents that sound; and (2) to print that letter enough times in association with its sound so that he can print (draw) it when he hears that sound.

When the child can hear and say several beginning sounds, select one—for example *h*. From among his sight-word 3x5 cards, select three or four words that begin with the letter *h*. Possibly *ham, hit* and *hop*. Lay the cards before him in a column:

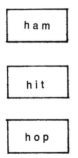

ham

hit

hop

Say each word. Have the child say each word. Say each again stressing the beginning *h* sound. Have the child repeat after you. Help the child realize that he is *starting to say* each of these words the same way with his mouth and voice. Ask the child if he *sees* anything that is the same about each of these three printed words. If he sees that all three begin with the same letter, praise him. If he doesn't see the similarity (give him time), place a sheet of paper over all three cards leaving only the first letter *h* exposed. Then, move the paper slowly off to the right. Repeat, if necessary.

When the child understands that the first letter is the same in each word *because* the beginning sound of each word is the same, tell him that is the letter (not the name of it, please) that *always* represents the beginning sound he has been making. Say it some more. Give him some paper and have him try copying just that letter several times. You can make a simple tracing model to help.

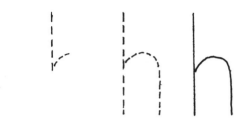

Have the child slowly trace the form of the letter with his finger a few times, then use a pencil. Allow all the practice he wants or needs, but don't extend the practice much past his real interest.

When the form of the first learned letter seems to be associated well with its appropriate sound and can be printed on paper, print it on one half of a 3x5 card as a neat model for him to keep at hand:

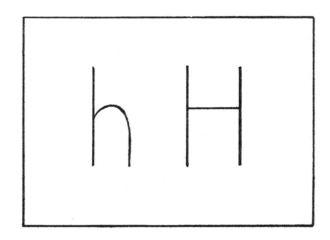

Give the child some paper and let him practice a lower-case *h* and a capital *H as a pair,* side by side, to help form a mental bond between the two. Have the child say the sound for *h* each time he prints either form of the letter.

You might think that the capital forms of letters should be learned later on, after all the lower-case forms are learned. But the child's world is full of capital letters. Though most book and magazine print is in lower case, much of the advertising a child sees is in capital letters entirely. When a child is with you at a traffic intersection, he will see a sign printed STOP. He won't see "stop." Even when he wants to know what comic-strip characters are saying, the print is in capitals.

To take advantage of the child's natural interest in print, which is all around him, you must introduce the capital letters as well as lower-case forms. Both must be taught. But stress the lower-case forms somewhat more in your sessions. Periodic reviews will help clinch the capital forms, in time.

Encourage the child to print as much as he desires. He'll become neater eventually. Be sure to save some of this early printing so the child can see his obvious progress over several weeks of practicing.

Learning the very first letter, with its particular sound, lower-case and capital forms, will take several sessions. Since the rest will be learned on this pattern and since the child will soon grasp the basic idea of sound-letter-print as a three-way mental combination, the process will speed up.

There is a logical general order for learning the consonant and short-vowel sounds. English as used in primary reading and in much of printing on signs that the child will see suggests the following groupings as a guide. The groupings are based on (1) the frequency with which certain letters appear in print, (2) their individuality of form, and (3) their potential value for early use in consonant-vowel-consonant words. Three-letter consonant-vowel-consonant words are going to be the simplest for you to use as you teach sound-letter associations. Table 4 on page 152 presents a list of easy short-sounded vowel words. Some of these should be among the first learned sight words.

Continue through the alphabet according to the following sequence of letters gradually repeating for each letter the learning process just described:

First-learned consonants	b m p t h r l
First-learned vowels	short-sound a i o
Next-learned consonants	f c n g d s w
Next-learned vowels	short-sound u e
Next-learned consonants	k j q v x y z

Table 5 on page 153 gives you a guide to letters for sounds. Once all short sounds for vowels are learned and are being used in words, you should introduce the long sounds for the vowels, gradually.

You need not exhaust the first group of consonants to be learned before taking up a couple of the short vowels. In fact, with three or four of the first group of consonants and a couple of the short vowels learned, you can show how letters, when re-arranged, make new words! This fact is the magic of printed language, *if* the reader knows the sounds of the letters!

Table 4

PHONEMICALLY REGULAR WORDS

Phonemically regular early sight words useful for teaching first letter, last letter and middle vowel sound-symbol associations, using only short-sound vowels:

ă		e		i		o		u	
can	cap	bed	beg	big	Bill	Bob	cog	bud	bug
cat	dad	bet	den	bit	did	cop	cot	bum	bun
Dan	fan	fed	fell	dig	dip	dog	doll	bus	but
fat	had	get	hen	fin	fit	Don	dot	cup	cut
has	hat	jet	leg	hid	his	God	got	dug	hug
lad	lap	let	men	hip	kid	fox	hog	hut	mud
mad	map	met	pen	hit	lid	job	mom	mug	mutt
nap	pad	pet	red	lip	mill	mop	nod	nut	pup
pan	pat	set	Ted	mix	pig	not	pot	putt	rub
ran	rat	tell	ten	pill	pin	rob	rod	rug	run
sad	sat	well	yell	rib	rip	rot	Tom	rut	sub
tag	tan	wet	yes	will	win	top	tot	sun	tub
man		yet		bin		toss		tug	

The child's first efforts at sounding out (phonetically decoding) an unknown three-letter word will be halting and may require your patience and encouragement. Give him help, but let him really try to use his own phonic skills. For the child to decode and say the first whole strange word successfully, so that he hears and recognizes what he says based on his own sound-letter knowledge, is a major accomplishment. This moment is cause for rejoicing and family praise. This event is comparable to

Table 5

SOUND-KEY WORDS

Initial Consonants

b as in bed, but
c as in cat, cut
c (soft) as in cent, city
d as in dog, dug
f as in fun, fish
g as in gun, go
g (soft) as in gentle
h as in hat, hut
j as in jar, jug
k as in key, kite
l as in let, lot
m as in man, met

n as in net, no
p as in pen, pan
q as in queen, quick
r as in run, ring
s as in sun, sing
t as in top, tin
v as in very, vine
w as in web, were
x as in x-ray
y as in year, yell
z as in zebra, zero

SOUND-KEY WORDS (*continued*)

Short Vowels

ă as in cat, map
e as in get, jet
i as in sit, hit
o as in not, got
u as in cut, nut

Long Vowels

ā as in ate, gate
ē as in me, be
ī as in nice, kite
ō as in go, no
ū as in use, mule

that moment when the child was learning to talk and he first realized that everything in the world has a name.

Your child now has a new insight into language. Have him print this first unknown word that he has actually *read*. Before proceeding, look over the summary of points that have been discussed so far in this chapter (Table 6).

REINFORCEMENT

In helping the child learn letters associated with sounds, you must do everything that will help reinforce and make the new learning more permanent. Saying a sound while looking at its letter helps to form the mental association needed. Saying the sound, looking at the letter and printing it help reinforce the association among all three things. Printing the lower-case form of the letter, saying the sound and printing the capital form of the letter extend the mental chain still further. Use every opportunity around the house and in the community to promote reinforcement (i.e., learning) of the letters with their sounds.

Table 6

LEARNING SOUNDS AND THEIR LETTERS

Activities

1. Hearing Sounds

—From the child's oral vocabulary select three or four short ·words that have different beginning, ending and middle sounds in them (all oral, no cards or print).

—Say you are going to play a game of careful listening.

—Have child repeat all after you.

—After saying the whole words naturally, slow down your rate of enunciation until the beginning sound of each word is emphasized; child repeats.

—Say just the beginning sound of a word; pause and say the whole word; child repeats.

—Continue practice until child can voice at least three or four different beginning sounds.

—Talk about words really being several sounds pushed together and that we can hear the separate sounds if we say the word slowly and listen.

—When the idea of separate sounds is understood, explain that printed letters tell us what sounds to say in reading.

—Say now he is ready to learn which letters show the sounds to say in words.

2. Learning Letters for Sounds

—Select three or four sight word cards with the same first letter.

—Show the 3x5 sight-word cards and pronounce them.

—Lay the cards before the child in a column.

—Point to each word and say it; emphasize the first sound of each word.

—Ask if the child can tell you what is the same about each word.

—Help child to see that the first letter is the same in each word.

—Say the beginning sound; child repeats.

—Say he is ready now to learn which letters represent sounds he makes when he says words and that this is the first letter he will learn (letter sound, not name!).

—Say the sound; point to the letter; child repeats.

—Repeat first sound and whole word; child repeats.

—When child says sound well and letter is known as representing that sound, print a model letter on paper and let child practice drawing it.

—Explain that all letters have two forms, little and big (lower case and capital); print the capital-form model and have child practice it, too; say sound at each printing.

—Practice lower case and capital alternately.

—Repeat for other beginning and ending sounds from first consonant group; carry out same activity for the other groups of letters progressively.

—Help child hear short vowel sounds in the middle of short words following the same pattern as above.

—Go through all the stages including printing vowels in lower-case and capital form.

—Review combinations to reinforce and check progress.

—Don't go to third group of letters without showing child he can really use his sound-letter-combination knowledge to figure out (decode, sound out, read) a word he does not yet know. Celebrate this achievement.

To help a child learn letters for sounds, tape a few cards showing a lower-case letter onto objects around the house. For example, tape the letter *l* onto a lamp. Tape a *t* onto the edge of a table; and an *r* on the radio, and so forth. Since the child knows the word for each household object, these letter tags will help remind him for a while that that object's *first sound* is that of the letter he sees taped there. You can have the child tell you letters for first sounds of other objects in the house.

Magazine pictures can be used in a similar manner to help forge the bond between a sound and its letter. Cut out pictures of objects and mark on each the appropriate first letter. Make a folder and use the pictures for the beginning sounds.

Not only are letters learned by sight, sound, writing and object association, but they can also be "experienced" in a three-dimensional way. Plastic or wooden letters can be purchased in various sizes. Even a cardboard cut-out letter can serve the purpose. Handling such letters, tracing around them and saying their sounds is another kind of reinforcement. Some children may find this useful if they have trouble printing. Even a typewriter in the house can be a means of letting the child search for a letter he recognizes, then striking it on the keyboard. Note, that the typewriter keys show letters in their capital forms but will type out in lower case unless you lock the capital-letter "hold" key into position first. Do so.

Use a shelf of books or canned goods to let your child look for letters he knows and show them to you. Be interested. Use any technique you can to encourage practice and to reinforce mental association of sounds and their respective letters. This is comparable to what you did day after day in teaching your child to learn to speak. Then, you seldom missed a chance to help him learn a new word through practice and by example. Surround him with the same intense climate for learning to read.

When a letter has been learned on sight, put up in his room or elsewhere a 3x5 card showing its lower case and capital forms. Add to this posting each time he has learned a new letter. Put up each card with pride—or have the child do it. Draw attention to the progress indicated by each addition. Have other members of the family praise the growing number of posted cards. Use the line of posted cards occasionally for review of sounds. He will think about letters more than you realize. The posted letters will "trigger" his language thinking during non-lesson time.

Learning any code requires constant practice. In time, letters become fixed in mind, but only with practice. Some will be temporarily forgotten more easily than others and must be recaptured. About every third or fourth session, concentrate on review and practice, to be sure that learning is being retained. Review also reassures the child as to how much he has learned and suggests how fast you can go with good results. The rate should be fast enough to actively continue new learning without frustration. Letters already learned require little practice. Don't bore the child. Learned letters will be reinforced as reading activity naturally increases.

WRITING AND READING

The object of learning *sight words* is to create a base for learning the beginning, ending and middle sounds in words and acquiring the ability to recognize and say *individual sounds*.

The object of learning individual sounds is to associate them mentally with the *letter form* each represents in print.

The object of learning individual letters associated with their sounds is to be able *to read*. This chain of progressive mental events, going from each newly known base to unknown symbols, is essential. It is the most direct and best route to travel. It works. Only the amount of time varies among children en route—just as it did in learning to talk.

Even when your child knows only a few sight words, a few consonants and a few short-sound vowels, he can begin to read in a new sense by using phonic skills. He should be made aware of reading by his sound-letter knowledge as soon as possible. This awareness will help him persist in learning additional letters and more sight words so that he can read more material with greater skill.

A by-product of learning letters for sounds will be learning to print. Up to now, his "reading" has been limited largely to whole sight words. While he is learning each letter form better by printing it, he is, in the process, also learning how to *write*.

Consider this printing practice as essential. Your child should have some printing practice with every sound-sight letter he is learning, before a new letter is taken up.

Writing out short stories that use words and letters the child knows is usually enjoyable. Have him tell you a short story. Print his story on a large sheet of paper or on the blackboard, substituting simple words (with his agreement) where necessary. When the story is complete (just three or four short sentences), read it to the child while moving your finger along under each word. Talk about the *idea* of the story. Suggest that he copy it and save it. Have him suggest a title for the story. Add it at the top. Have the child print his name as author at the bottom. Date it. These sheets can be the start of a "library" of his own work. Pride of authorship will be self-reinforcing. It is not necessary that the child know every word you have printed in his dictated story.

Other logical features of printed language may emerge as soon as you are working with thoughts in short sentences. You may need to explain the question mark and the period and their use. Do so, briefly.

As you work with letters and the child does more printing, you may need to explain how adding an *s* at the end of a word that names an object usually makes the word mean more than one of the object named. Or, you may need to talk about some other unexpected feature, such as a final *-ed* on a verb or an *-ing* ending. When the child's interest raises a point naturally, comment matter-of-factly and go on with the planned object of the session. Do not reject any question of natural interest, even though its specific development will not come until later. Treat questions naturally and briefly, and continue. You don't have to try to explain the whole thing now. Be direct and courteous in response to the child's inquiries, and get on with your main plan.

You have been working with four mental processes as you helped your child start with just his oral vocabulary. What you have done mentally for the child has been to help him

1. to associate words he speaks
   with corresponding whole w

2. to become aware of the in
   sight words that he speaks;

3. to associate individual so
   letters in print as each c

4. to apply his sound-let
   reading unknown print

The summary in Table 7 provides a revie.
activities you must guide to develop the basic reading
your preschooler.

Table 7

PRINTING AND READING

Activities

1. Printing (writing)

—Child prints each letter as he learns which sound it represents; secure practice in lower-case and in capital-letter
form.

—Make a letter card to post for each letter when learned;
show lower-case and capital forms on same card.

—Praise child and emphasize progress; use posted cards for
occasional review.

—Consider printing as essential activity.

—Have child dictate a simple story; copy it on large paper;
read it together; discuss the idea of it.

—Have child copy story; add title; have child sign name.

—Experiment with words child might like to try to copy—
even long ones.

—Encourage printing from memory where possible.

—Encourage correct holding of writing instrument.

—Note sequence and direction of letter stroking from Appendix B.

...eading (decoding)
—Continue to enlarge sight-word knowledge.
—Stress sound-letter knowledge; apply as learned to words that use just letters child knows.
—Require some decoding practice regularly.
—Work with longer sentences by mixing sight words with unknown words child can decode.
—Be generous with your help, but always allow time for child to work out decoding by himself.
—Take child into community watching for signs; praise any word recognition.
—Leave magazines and large-print reading material easily in reach at home.
—Begin to buy books that child wants; look over several; let child select (even slightly beyond his ability).
—Visit the local library; explain and use it.
—Continue reading for fun to the child daily.
—Continue 20-minute-daily sessions; consider adding another 20-minute session in the other half day.
—Buy, borrow or make up as many books and stories as the child will read.
—Learning to read is for reading; make it possible.

3. Managing Sounds and Letters
—Use only letters for which sounds are already known.
—Cut up a 3x5 card into 1x3 strips; print one learned letter on each strip in lower-case form; make several of each as learned, for later practice use.
—Think about how you can make the idea understood that when letters are rearranged they make new words *because* the sounds will be voiced in a different order.
—Change the beginning, the ending and the middle sounds one at a time until the idea is grasped.
—Select three sight-word cards of only three letters each, all of which are known to the child.

—Place one card before the child; name it; sound it out; select the three strips with the letters that spell that word; arrange strips right below the sight-word card; agree with child that the two words are the same.

—Remove only the first letter strip and replace it with another consonant letter strip, the sound for which the child knows and which will make another word; ask child what the word says now; allow thinking time; encourage sounding effort.

—Replace former beginning letter and say word; substitute the new strip and have the child try the new word; if necessary, tell the new word; repeat the changed beginning letter and word sounds.

—Repeat with other words and change beginning letters until child grasps the idea that a changed beginning letter changes the first sound and therefore the whole word in sound and meaning.

—Repeat the process for ending letters and sounds.

—Repeat the process for middle-letter sounds (short-vowel sounds only at first).

—As child's knowledge increases, continue to make words from his letter strips and rearrange letters; point out that short vowel generally has to be inside a word; go to all short vowels as soon as possible.

—Make a lot of letter strips and let child see how many words he can make and show you later; leave him alone with strips to experiment.

—Be generous with your praise.

—Try dictating a few words for child to print; enunciate clearly and slowly; select words to assure initial success.

—Put partial words on chalkboard or on paper, and add a first or last letter to make new words—e.g., _at, *m*at, *h*at, *b*at; or use ma_ to become ma*p*, ma*t*, ma*d*, etc.

THE READING PRESCHOOLER

If you have followed the plan outlined in this book, your child is reading by now. He may be ahead of your expectations or a little behind. Various factors could affect the progress. A bright three-year-old, a typical four-year-old and a slower five-year-old could show quite similar reading skills from the same over-all exposure to these experiences. In any case, they all would have learned to read at a level not ordinarily to be expected until after the first grade.

Most importantly, you have guaranteed that learning to read will not be a confusing or upsetting experience for your child in school. When he enters the first grade, tell your child's teacher that you have worked with him and show some material he now reads easily. The teacher will go on from that point.

You have provided the important introduction to learning to read *at the natural time* of the child's interest in printed language. You have dealt successfully with many of the regular features of learning to read. Irregular features will be taken up at school later. Reading is a complex skill that will continue to develop and unfold over several years. But you have laid the important foundation already for the child's permanent success.

Depending on when you started, how soon the child will enter first grade, and what level of reading skill he now shows, there are a number of other skill refinements that you are quite capable of teaching at home. If there is time, continue to help your child. Even though he may be in school, you can continue his reading instruction productively.

10
Extending
Basic
Reading Skills

Learning to read is for reading. Encourage your child to read a word, a label, an ad, a sign—anything. His reading skills will continue to improve, and the usefulness of what he reads will increase. Decoding even one word independently helps to make the child aware of his budding reading power. Make buying a book in the local supermarket or elsewhere a special event, but a regular one. Let the child browse through what is available. Let the choice be his whenever possible.

The skills you have been drawing out of the child have been those of *beginning reading*. They are the most fundamental and require the most patience and persistence. Progress is dramatic, though, within a few months. The exhilaration and satisfaction of achievement are also the greatest.

It is on the foundation of basic reading skills that a lifetime of productive and satisfying reading rests. The child's skill in reading will continue to grow and improve for many years. Your role has been to open the gate of his mind to reading at the time he was naturally ready and most motivated to learn the basic elements. You have enhanced the likelihood that he will use and enjoy reading all his life and that he will not become a casualty of starting too late or be harmed by poor reading instruction or neglect in a beginning-reading class at school.

Though you could stop at this point with satisfaction, it may be several months before your child enters the first grade. Use them. There are a number of further steps that you can take—even after he has entered first grade. At the very least, you will want to continue regular recreational reading daily at home. More sight words can be learned with profit. Reviewing recently learned skills in sounds, letters and printing will help to establish full mastery. Your child will not want to discontinue reading-skill sessions and using printing, even though he may have achieved all of the skills suggested up to this point.

If your child has mastered most of the previously described skills and if time remains, even if he has entered first grade, you can work with him on the following additional points. These are the next-most-regular features of English that he can profitably learn.

CONTINUING WITH YOUR FIVE-YEAR-OLD

Before you decide to advance your child's reading further, it would be useful to be sure that the skills outlined up to this point are well fixed in his mind. These will assure him of success in formal reading at school.

You have the personal security that you have largely removed the one-in-four chance that your child could become a handicapped reader later on. Also, under the plan of this book, you have made his early reading experiences natural, interesting and satisfying. You have spared your child the emotional anxiety and neglect that many children suffer in learning to read in groups in the primary grades.

Before you work on more skills, you should check your child's basic mastery. If any deficiency is located, it should receive attention first. Consolidating past gains is your first responsibility. From work to date, your child should

1. know a good variety of sight words;
2. know all the consonant sounds and their letters;
3. know the short-vowel sounds and their letters;

4. know the long sounds for the same vowels;
5. know the lower-case and capital forms of letters and correctly print each from models (some from memory);
6. know the letter sounds and print most letters on request;
7. know the letter names through incidental learning;
8. know how to decode simple unknown words using phonic skills;
9. know how to substitute letters in words to make new words;
10. write simple stories with satisfaction;
11. read simple stories with satisfaction;
12. use reading skills in many out-of-home situations.

The above list of skills is aimed at being certain that your child

1. has a sight-word vocabulary;
2. knows the basic sound-letter combinations;
3. knows and can print letters;
4. can apply phonic skills to word analysis (decoding);
5. understands the principle of interchangeability of letters in our printed code;
6. can apply his reading skill in reading and writing as a practical and satisfying tool, which is the object of the entire effort.

If you have been natural but opportunistic with your child in basic-reading training over the past few months, you have probably already answered some questions that are involved in extending his basic-reading skill. You may only need, therefore, to review some points briefly, or they may be entirely new. For example, you likely have talked with your child about an added final *s* on nouns, or an *s* or *ing* ending on verbs. In regard to certain sight words, you probably have found it necessary to talk briefly about words that begin with two consecutive consonant letters and the sound they make together. An example of such beginning consonant "blends" are *bl, cl, gr,* et cetera. These additional features of words and reading can be usefully studied now.

LOGICAL NEXT STEPS

During the past year you have been working with regular and consistent features of our printed code. Because of these regular features you have been able to make good progress in basic reading. The problems some words present by irregular spellings and nonsensical sounds if decoded literally have been circumvented by learning them as whole sight words.

A few other fairly regular features of the language can be learned at home. Soon, however, a number of inconsistencies must be dealt with and will be better taken up at school. The first inconsistency you have dealt with so far was short and long sounds for the same vowels. In that case the child had to learn that the same letter may represent two different sounds. Without learning arbitrary language rules, he knows enough to try one or the other of the two sounds and that the short sound will be the right one in most words. His ear will usually tell him which is right. Another inconsistency was learned when you showed the child that each letter can be printed in two ways—in lower case and in capital form. These are only the first of many inconsistencies in English.

For the rest of his life your child will learn sight words. You, yourself, read mostly by sight-word knowledge. When was the last time you consciously "sounded out" a word? Continue to enlarge the child's sight vocabulary. As an adult he will read almost entirely by instant recognition of sight words. So-called "speed reading" would not be possible otherwise, since whole phrases are engulfed at a single eye fixation in that process. Even average rates of adult reading do not involve stopping for phonetic analysis. Just now, though, your child's sight vocabulary is a very important source of words to help in learning phonic decoding principles. You should continue to develop a sight vocabulary up to as many as 300 words.

The remaining skills you can develop with the child before he enters first grade deal with (1) compound words; (2) alternate sounds for *c* and *g*; (3) sounds for words starting with two consonants; and (4) common endings of words. These are generally consistent features, but they require the same careful attention, practice and use that developed the earlier skills. Table 8 lists these remaining skills for extending your child's reading and decoding talents before he enters the first grade.

Table 8

ELEMENTS IN EXTENDING BASIC READING

Compound Words

cowboy	softball
anything	backyard
houseboat	without
horseback	nowhere

Alternate Sounds for *c* and *g*

hard *c* as in cat, cart, candy
hard *g* as in go, get, gas
soft "c" as in city, cell, circus
soft "g" as in giant, general, George

Initial Consonant Combinations

two-letter *blends* that start words (two sounds blended)
    l blends—*bl, cl, fl, gl, pl, sl,*
    r blends—*br, cr, fr, gr, pr, tr*
    other blends—*sc, sm, sn, sk, sp, st*
two-letter *digraphs* that start words (sounded as one)
    ch, sh, th, wh, sw

Common Endings

s added to nouns (dog, dogs; boy, boys; hat, hats)
s added to verbs (put, puts; sit, sits; work, works)
ed added to verbs (jump, jumped; pull, pulled; walk, walked)
ing added to verbs (sing, singing; call, calling)

Possessive *'s* for Ownership

the boy's hat
Tom's coat
the chair's leg

Compound Words

If you have not talked with your child specifically about compound words yet, do so. Very likely he has discovered a word as part of another word already. However, just any word within the spelling of another word does not produce a compound word. Two whole words, each of which is identifiable and can be pronounced separately, but which make a new meaning when joined together as one word, form a compound word. There are many examples.

Use a story or write several sentences on the blackboard using compound words. Read the story. Reread the words distinctly so the child will discover the nature of the compound words. Think up others and write them on the board. Have the child sort through his sight-word cards to see if two can be joined to make a compound word. See how long a list can be made over several days.

Alternate Sounds for *c* and *g*

When you helped your child understand that the letters *a*, *e*, *i*, *o* and *u*—the vowels—could each have two sounds (short and long), you laid the foundation for understanding that a few other letters occasionally do the same. The usual ones are *c* and *g*. Later on, in school, he will learn other peculiarities of some letters such as sounds for *y*, final *e*, and special spellings to produce sounds for the letters *k*, *f*, *s*, *z* and *j* and how double-vowel letters are sounded. If you help him with just the other sound for *c* and *g* now, though, that is enough before first grade.

In sight words he knows already that there are examples of the so-called hard and soft sounds for *c* and *g*. He learned the hard-*c* sound originally. Select several words starting with the letter *c* sounded each way. Hard *c* is sounded like a *k*, as in cat. Soft *c* is sounded like an *s*, as in city. Write out a short story in which the words use both types of sounds for *c*. Read the story. Call attention to the *c* starting words. Say them alone. See if the child hears a different first sound. Distinguish between the two different beginning sounds. Have the child find some more *c* starting words among his sight-word cards and sort them into two piles to show the two different sounds that a beginning *c* can make. Is there anything alike about the spelling of hard-sounding *c*-starting words? Soft-sounding *c* words?

The child will likely see among his sight words that hard *c* usually has the vowel *a, o* or *u* after it. Soft *c* usually has an *e* or *i* after it. These sounds can also occur inside a word. If a child is stuck in decoding a *c* word sometime, he should remember to try both sounds, as he does for short and long vowel sounds already.

Hard and soft *g* parallel hard and soft *c*. Follow the same procedure as above with *g*-starting words that illustrate both of its sounds. After you work around to sorting out two piles of sight words that illustrate the two sounds of *g*, the child will draw the same conclusion that hard *g* is usually followed by the vowels *a, o* or *u*, and soft *g*, with the *j* sound, is usually followed by *e* or *i*. Watch to see if the child applies these two options for sounds in his reading. Remind him about the two sounds for *c* and *g*, as necessary.

Initial Consonant Combinations

Among the usual words found in primary readers and early story materials are those that start with two consecutive consonant letters that are *blended* together when they are sounded in words. Elements of both initial consonant sounds are present, as in saying *bl*ue, *bl*ack, *br*own, *gr*een, *gl*ass, *gr*ow. About two dozen pairs of consonants start words this way. Over half of them have either *l* or *r* as the second letter to be blended with the first letter. Most of the others have the letter *s* as the first letter followed by various second-letter consonants (see Table 9).

Arrange for the child to practice blending the *l* and *r* combinations. Write a story on the blackboard including various *l* and *r* blends. Read the story. Stress the initial sounds of the two

Table 9

INITIAL CONSONANT COMBINATIONS

Initial Consonant Blends

l blends

bl as in blue	**gl** as in glad
cl as in club	**pl** as in play
fl as in flag	**sl** as in slow

r blends

br as in brake	**fr** as in frozen
cr as in cross	**gr** as in green
dr as in drink	**pr** as in price

Other blends

sc as in score	**st** as in stand
sk as in skate	**sw** as in swing
sm as in small	**tr** as in train
sn as in snail	**tw** as in twin
sp as in spring	

Initial Consonant Digraphs

sh as in show	**th** as in that
ch as in chance	**wh** as in what
gh as in ghost	

blended consonants. Identify the two letters that are blended. Have the child repeat and stress them. With that model, sort through the sight-word cards to find other words that start the same way. Make a list of them on the board. See and say each, so that the blended sound becomes fixed. Copy and say several times. Say the blended sound and have the child print the two letters. Spend a little time on *s*-starting words that have an initial blend sound; but don't insist on mastery, now.

Other pairs of initial consonants frequently start common words your child knows. In this case, the first two consonant letters are sounded *as one sound*. Usually, the letter *h* is the second letter. Such common words as *th*e, *th*en, *wh*o, *wh*ere, *sh*ow, *sh*ine, *ch*ange, *ch*ance illustrate the point. The two starting sounds are merged into *one* sound. Such a combination is one example of a digraph. But don't bother the child with the term *digraph*.

Write a story on the blackboard, using several words that present a beginning digraph. Read the story together. Call attention to the digraph words. Stress the combined beginning sound. Have the child repeat until he is conscious of its nature with different first letters paired with the second letter *h*. Again, sort through the sight-word cards looking for examples of each beginning digraph. List them on the board, grouped according to their own digraph. Have the child say and copy each list for practice.

Word Endings

The best clues for phonic analysis usually are found at the start of a word. The way you have worked with your child and the suggestions offered have emphasized the way words begin. Even though attention has not been called to endings, other than final consonant sounds, you have surely commented about some word ending before now in your reading sessions. Four common endings should be examined.

Adding the letter *s* to a noun to make it mean more than one—i.e., *plural*—is the most common added ending. The child probably knows this already, but you should be sure. Use the blackboard with several examples. Have him add an *s* to change the meaning of nouns in a sentence and explain to you the meaning of the change. Note, this will be a good opportunity to point out that changing one part of a sentence can make it necessary to change another part. For example, the verb in the sentence may need to be changed when the noun is made plural. But don't labor over these matters. Comment on them and proceed with the purpose you have in mind.

Print singular and plural forms of the same noun. Write a sentence with a blank space in which to enter only one form. Ask the child which noun form should be used. Have him draw a line under his choice. If correct, write it in the space. If incorrect, discuss it. Practice, as needed.

You may comment that *es* is added when the noun already ends in *s* in its singular form as in *kiss, kisses*. Without belaboring the point, you should mention that not all names of things become plural by just adding *s*. Go through the sight-word cards deciding how to make singular forms into their plural forms. There are some special words that we must memorize—such as man, men; foot, feet.

Verbs in sentences are the words that describe the action and tell when it occurs. The change in time of action usually is indicated by changing the ending of the verb. The child already uses the common endings for verbs in his speech. Some of his sight words show those endings. Take up the common endings, *s, ed,* and *ing*.

Add *s* to some sight words (verbs) on the blackboard. Use the *s*-ending verb in several sentences orally. Have the child repeat them orally. Decide that the *s*-ending action word is used when you are talking about a person or a thing doing something *now*—"he jumps," "it jumps," "Tom jumps," "the frog jumps," and so forth. Try it orally with other subjects such as "I jumps," "you jumps," "we jumps" or "they jumps," and decide that the *s*-ending verb *sounds right* only when it is used to describe what some *other* individual person or thing does (i.e., third person singular—he, she, it). Emphasize *what sounds right* to the child rather than state a rule. If the child seems unsure, provide practice in saying the verb correctly rather than writing it. When he learns to say the verb and sentence correctly it will be written correctly, later.

Adding a final *ed* to a verb clearly changes the time of the action described. Use the final *s* and a final *ed* for the same word orally and then on the blackboard—that is, print out "he jumps," "he jumped," and so forth. Can the child tell you the difference meant by the time of the action due to the different endings? If not, explain it to him. Use examples, discuss and practice until the child understands the difference between the two kinds of endings. The *ed* can be used with any subject; not just with the "he," "she" and "it" subjects. Use the blackboard and sentences to

fix the use in context. Again, you must point out that some words
that are action words don't use the *ed* ending and will be memo-
rized in time. For example, *run, ran; sing, sang.* Using *ed* on the
verb, if possible, clearly means the action has already taken
place.

An *ing* is another common ending for verbs. However, this
ending (a suffix) to a word appears in several ways in English so
don't present it as though it just applied to verbs. Use the ending
on several verbs in sentences. Have the child repeat and make
new suggestions. Does he have any sight-word cards with these
final three letters? Are some not verbs? When *ing* is a natural part
of the one spelling of the word it isn't a verb—for example,
"thing," "wing," "nothing." Adding *ing* to a verb requires the
prior use of some form of the verb *to be* in the same sentence, to
give meaning—for example, "he *is* jumping"; "the boy *was* jumping"; "I *am* jumping." The *ing* added to the verb indicates that
the action continued for some time whenever it did occur (or will
occur—"I *will be* jumping"). So, *ing* may be a natural part of
some words or, in the case of verbs or action words, it may be
added to show a different time and duration of the action taking
place. (Note: The *ing* ending may be added to noun forms such
as "a building," "a landing"; or it may be used as the ending on
participial adjectives such as a "galloping horse," a "dressing
room," etc.)

One more ending involving the letter *s* is its use with the
apostrophe (') to show possession or ownership. When *'s* is
added to the name of a person or a thing, it conveys the idea of
possession—e.g., "Tom's dog," "Bill's ball"; or "the chair's leg,"
"the rug's color." The uniqueness of form of the apostrophe
makes this symbol quickly recognized. Practice its use on the
blackboard. Select noun sight words and use short sentences to
show how adding the *'s* means that something else in the sentence belongs to that word (the dog belongs to Tom; the leg to
the chair, and the color to the rug).

A period and a question mark should be used and understood
by now.

READY FOR FIRST GRADE

Beyond this point so many rules and exceptions enter into developing further phonic, spelling and reading skills that progress is better left to the teacher at school and the variety of helping materials she can use. Already, you can see the exceptions needing to be noted or explained when you talked about *ing* as a verb ending, as a natural part of another word, the necessity for some form of the verb *to be* to precede an *ing*-ending verb somewhere in the sentence, and other exceptions. At this stage of reading development we are passing out of the realm of beginning- and basic-reading skills and away from the regular features of English that you can easily teach at home.

If you have helped your child consistently within the framework of the goals and activities suggested in this book, you have prepared him to enter first grade as a successful beginning reader. You have satisfied his natural desire to know what the printed code is about, and you have developed his ability to understand and to use the basic symbols of printed English.

You have unlocked the mystery of the printed code and you have prepared your child basically to be a successful reader for the rest of his life.

Finally, this is no small feat that you have accomplished. Except for your conviction about your child's ability and your willingness to ignore the historic age-six myth, you might never have started. Though you knew you had taught your child human speech, you still had a corner of real doubt in your mind that maybe teaching beginning reading might be a different matter. But, by taking time almost daily, confidently and patiently, within the framework of this book, you have drawn the child out and you have created a beginning reader successfully. What greater gift could you bestow on your child?

APPENDIX A

FORMING LETTERS

The first step in forming letters is holding the pencil properly. Have the child hold the pencil comfortably between his thumb and third finger at a place about one inch above the writing point. Place the index finger over and on the pencil. Do not grip too tightly. Keep the wrist relatively flat rather than on its side.

The child should practice the lower-case and capital forms of each letter as it is being learned. A base line on which to write each letter may be used. Practice uniformity of size *after* the shape of each letter is mastered.

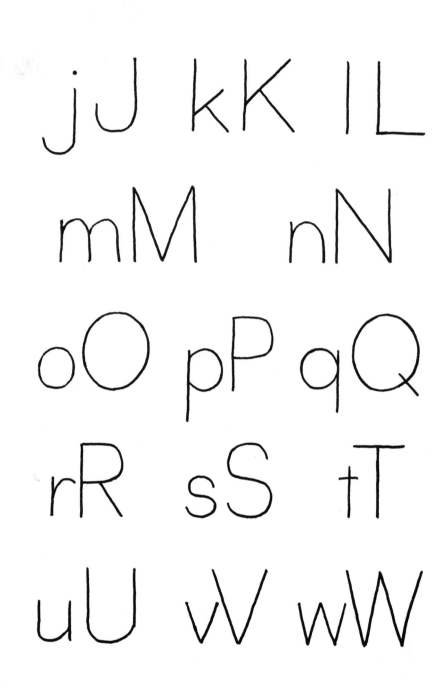

jJ kK lL

mM nN

oO pP qQ

rR sS tT

uU vV wW

xX yY zZ

FORMING NUMBERS

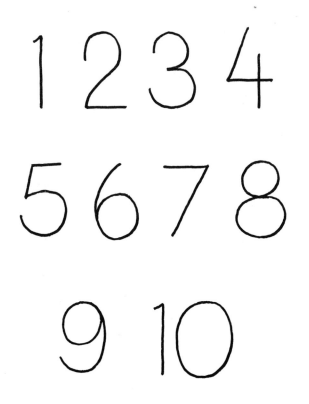

1 2 3 4

5 6 7 8

9 10

APPENDIX B

STROKING SEQUENCE FOR THE LETTERS

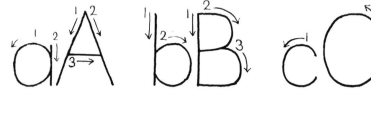

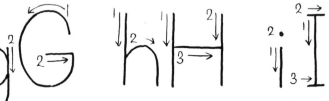

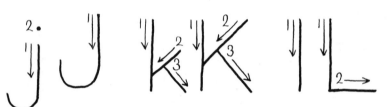

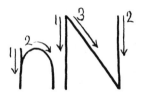

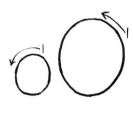

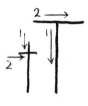

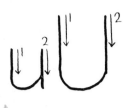

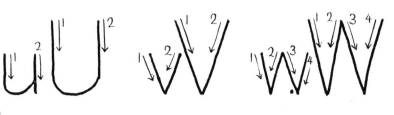

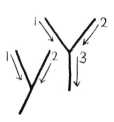

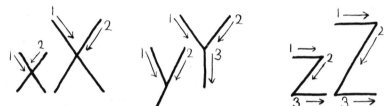

NOTES

1. The Myth, Our Language and Literacy.

1. National Advisory Committee on Dyslexia and Related Reading Disorders, *Reading Disorders in the United States.* Chicago: Developmental Learning Materials, 1969.
2. Martin, G. H., *The Evolution of the Massachusetts Public School System.* New York: Appleton, 1898, pp. 8–9.
3. Morphett, Mabel V., and Washburne, C., "When Should a Child Begin to Read?" *Elementary School Journal,* Vol. 31 (1931), pp. 496–503.
4. Pei, Mario, *The Story of Language,* revised edition. New York: New American Library, 1965, p. 312.

2. Learning to Talk—Grasping the Great Idea.

1. Brackbill, Yvonne, ed., *Infancy and Early Childhood.* New York: The Free Press, Macmillan, 1967, p. 311.
2. Pei, Mario, *op. cit.,* p. 124.
3. *Ibid.*
4. Dewey, Godfrey, *Relativ Frequency of English Speech Sounds,* Cambridge, Massachusetts: Harvard University Press, 1923, p. 19.
5. Hurlock, Elizabeth B., *Child Development,* fourth edition. New York: McGraw-Hill, 1956, p. 247.

3. The Remarkable Senses—Ready to Go.

1. Mental age refers to the usual level of native intelligence for a child of given chronological age.
2. National Society for the Study of Education, *Development in and Through Reading,* Sixtieth Yearbook. Chicago: Chicago University Press, 1961, p. 21.
3. Lindquist, E. F., ed., *Educational Measurement.* Washington, D.C.: American Council on Education, 1951, p. 11.
4. Sinclair, Ward, Miller, Mary L., and Alexander, Donald K., *Status of Reading Certification in the United States.* Washington, D.C.: American Federation of Teachers, 1970.
5. California State Department of Public Health, *Hearing Testing of School Children.* Berkeley, January 1962, p. 9.
6. *Ibid.*
7. Jaubenhous, Leon J., and Jackson, Anne A., *Vision Screening of Pre-School Children.* Springfield, Illinois: Charles C. Thomas, 1969, p. viii.

8. Hirsch, Monroe J., O.D., and Wiek, Ralph E., O.D., eds., *Vision of Children, An Optometric Symposium.* Philadelphia and New York: Chilton Books, 1963, p. 75.

9. *Ibid.*

10. Gesell, Arnold, *The First Five Years of Life.* New York: Harper & Brothers, 1940, p. 46.

11. *Ibid.*, p. 46.

12. *Ibid.*, p. 89.

4. Reading Four-Year-Olds

1. Durkin, Dolores, *Children Who Read Early.* New York: Teachers College Press, 1966.

2. Selected from the 1958 edition of the Gates Reading Tests, *Primary Word Recognition* and *Primary Paragraph Reading.*

3. Interpret these scores as: 1.9 means achieving at the ninth-month level of the first grade (i.e., at a level to be expected in May of the first-grade year of school).

4. *Ibid.*, Appendix A, p. 151.

5. Ebel, Robert L., ed., *Encyclopedia of Educational Research,* fourth edition. London: Collier-Macmillan, 1969, p. 325.

6. McKee, Paul, and Brezinski, Joseph E., *The Effectiveness of Teaching Reading in Kindergarten.* Cooperative Research Project No. 5–0371. Denver: The Denver Public Schools, 1966.

7. *Ibid.*, p. 84.

8. *Ibid.*, p. 90.

9. Davidson, Helen P., "An Experimental Study of Bright, Average and Dull Children at the Four-Year Mental Level," *Genetic Psychology Monograph,* Vol. IX, Nos. 3–4. Worcester, Mass.: Clark University, March-April, 1931, pp. 123–289.

10. As scored by the Pressy First Grade Reading Test.

11. Montessori, Maria, *The Discovery of the Child,* translated by M. Joseph Costelloe, S.J. New York: Ballantine Books, 1967, p. 199.

12. *Ibid.*, p. 226.

13. *Ibid.*, p. 229.

14. *Ibid.*, p. 233.

15. *Ibid.*, p. 234.

16. Bruce, Addington H., ed., *The Education of Karl Witte.* New York: Thomas Y. Crowell, 1914.

5. Why Not Just Wait?

1. Bloom, Benjamin S., *Stability and Change in Human Characteristics.* New York: John Wiley & Sons, 1964.

2. *Ibid.,* p. 68.

6. *Deciding to Start with Your Pre-School Child*
1. A study involving primary- and elementary-grade children in the
   South San Francisco Unified School District demonstrated that
   even the I.Q. scores of children selected at random could be
   raised over the school year if the teacher had been *told* that
   unpredictable academic spurts of progress could be expected in
   these children. See Robert Rosenthal and Lenore Jacobson,
   Pygmalion in the Classroom, New York, Holt, Rinehart and
   Winston, 1968.
2. Aukerman, Robert C., *Approaches to Beginning Reading.* New
   York: John Wiley and Sons, 1971.
3. Chall, Jeanne, *Learning to Read: The Great Debate.* New York:
   McGraw-Hill, 1967.

7. *What Is the Best Plan?*
1. Bond, Guy L., and Dykstra, Robert, *Final Report of the Coordinating Center for First-Grade Reading Instruction Programs,* U.S.
   Department of Health, Education and Welfare, Office of Education, Bureau of Research. Minneapolis: University of Min-
   nesota, 1967.
2. Bruner, Jerome, *The Process of Education.* Cambridge, Massachusetts: Harvard University Press, 1960, p. 32.

INDEX

Ability grouping, based on performance levels, 101

Activities
  involved in developing sight vocabulary (table), 144
  involved in learning sounds and their letters (table), 154
  involved in printing (table), 159
  passive language, 36, 37

Adult population, median level of formal schooling of, 93

Age-six myth
  facts disproving, 65
  grounds supporting, 62
  influence of compulsory attendance laws on, 19–20
  influence of testing on, 20–22
  irrationality of, 117
  parents and, 17, 18, 22, 23, 66
  perpetuation of, 17–18
  as unquestioned, 119

Alphabet, order of learning sounds for, 146, 151

Articulation, as readiness indicator, 105

Assessment of readiness
  of child, 104–07
  of parent, 111–15

Attention span
  as readiness indicator, 106–7
  as secondary readiness characteristic, 133

Attention-giving, speech development and, 35

Babbling, 35, 44

Basal-reader series approach, 120–122

Basic reading skills, 163–74

Beginning-reading instruction
  clues indicating time to start, 90
  effects of compulsory attendance laws on, 20
  effects of delaying, 18
  intelligence and, 91
  mass media and, 73–74
  maturational theory of development and, 87–89

Beginning-reading instruction (*Cont.*)
  in nursery schools, 95–98
  optimal time for, 86; *see also* Teachable moment
  reading materials available, 92
  See also First-grade reading instruction; Home-reading instruction

Beginning sounds of words, 147

Black English, 42

Bloom, Benjamin S., 91

Brain deficiencies, 51

Brain development, 50–51

Bruner, Jerome, 127

Checklist for starting home-reading instruction, 132–33

Chicago Tribune (newspaper), 74

Child development, maturational theory of, 65, 80, 87–89

Class size in first grade, 100

Code emphasis, defined, 118

Common endings of words, dealing with (table), 167

Compound words
  dealing with (table), 167, 168
  recognition vocabulary increased by, 33

Comprehension, as readiness indicator, 107

Compulsory attendance laws
  based on social readiness, 47
  effects of, on age-six myth, 19–20
  pseudo-scientific halo of mental age and, 22

Consonants, 148, 151 (table), 153
  initial consonant combinations, 167 (table), 169, 170 (table), 171

Continuous progress primary grades (nongraded primary grades), 101

Cooing, as first verbal activity, 35

Copying, 50, 59, 61, 62
  home environment conducive to, 82, 83